UPRISING:
"WE ARE THE REVOLUTION."

By Randy L. Noble
with
Heather Joy

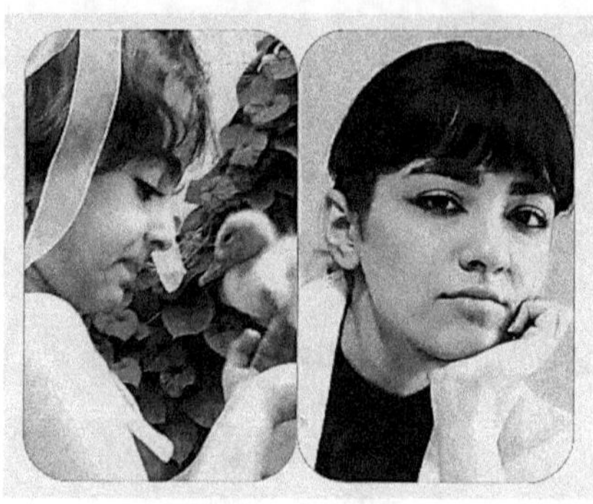

Nika Shakarami (pictured here to the left) as a young, innocent child enjoying life. On September 20, 2022, Nika was brutally murdered by security forces in the city of Tehran. Her crime? Peacefully protesting for freedom! *She was only 16.*
#NeverforgetNika.

The famous slogan, "*Woman, life, freedom,*" has given birth to a powerful, indestructible female-led movement in Iran that is "hell bent" on overthrowing a dictatorship government that has oppressed their human rights for more than forty years. Iranian women are not just protesting the *Hijab Law* or a "few strands of hair." These courageous women are fighting for freedom, justice, and democracy against a deadly gender-apartheid system!

It is the absolute passion of my life to be a voice for my dear Iranian friends. The Bible instructs me to be a voice of hope and freedom for them.

"Open your mouth for the mute, for the rights of all who are destitute,
Open your mouth, judge righteously,
Defend the rights of the poor and needy."

(Proverbs 31:8-9, ESV translation)

"Speak up for those who cannot speak for themselves.
Ensure justice for those being crushed.
Yes, speak up for the poor and helpless and see that they get justice."

(Proverbs 31:8-9, NIV translation)

There is a powerful, little Psalm that God has put on my heart to use in my daily prayer time for my Iranian friends. I have posted it in almost every book that I have written. This psalm has become the passionate cry of my heart to God that He will deliver them from the oppression and fear of a dictatorship government. I am confident that the evil foundation of this current regime has many cracks in it and God is about to crush it!

"He will rescue the poor when they cry to him: He will help the oppressed, who have no one to defend them.
He feels pity for the weak and the needy, and he will rescue them.
He will redeem them from oppression and violence, for their lives are precious to him."

(Psalm 72:12-14, NLT translation)

I know God hears the cries of my heart for my dear Iranian friends. *Daniel 2:20 declares:* "He controls the course of world events: He removes kings and sets up other kings." God is sovereign and at the appointed time, He will bring this evil government to their knees and avenge the Iranian people.

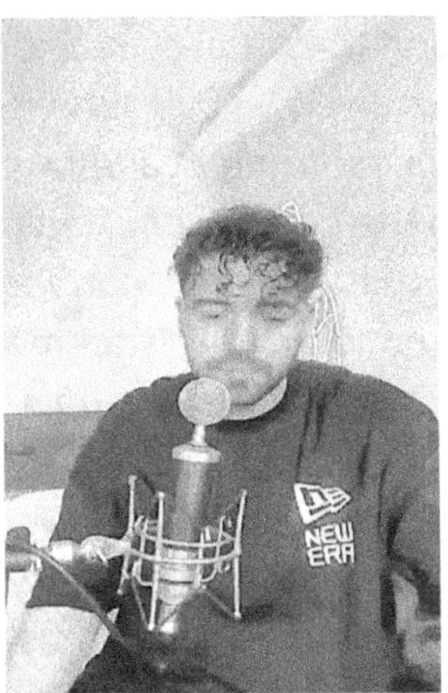

<u>Shervin Hajipour's Anthem for the uprising</u>

Iranian artist, Shervin Hajipour, never dreamed that his two-and-a-half-minute ballad would be watched on Instagram by more than 60 million viewers. Gathering comments from online tweets, Shervin composed an emotional song about Iranians angry at an oppressive government and desperately yearning for a better life whose children were forced to "pick through the trash in search of their dreams."

Just eleven days after the unjust death of Mahsa Amini, Shervin posted a video of himself singing, "Baraye" on Instagram. The video immediately went viral! He was arrested just two days later and forced to remove the popular video and shut down his Instagram account. The 25-year-old singer was summoned to the police station charged with encouraging riots and acting against national security.

Despite being arrested and forced to remove the video, his song, "Baraye" refused to die in the hearts of Iranians and people all over the world. "Baraye" soon became an anthem song for worldwide protests and rallies. By October 1, crowds of Iranians around the world in over 200 cities, marched through the streets singing along to the lyrics of the song.

"But it didn't stop there!"

People began calling for Hajipour's song to be nominated for a

Grammy in the "best song for social change," category. Almost immediately, "Baraye" received 95,000 submissions for a Grammy award, according to the Recording Academy. Shervin had found a profound connection in the hearts of millions of people putting a "face" on the sufferings of Iranians. Recording Academy CEO, Harvey Mason Jr, declared in a public statement, "*The Academy steadfastly supports freedom of expression and art that's created to empower communities in need. Because music serves the world, and the Recording Academy exists to serve music.*"

Responding to intense worldwide pressure, Shervin Hajipour was released on bail on October 4, facing charges of *spreading propaganda against the regime and encouraging and inciting people to acts of violence* and will stand trial in the near future. The Islamic Republic of Iran is notorious for squelching freedom of expression in the arts and has in the past imprisoned musicians, film directors, and dancers. Shervin Hajipour is one more example of this regime's desperate attempt to control the minds of talented musicians who pose a threat to their existence.

Since "Baraye" was written and sung in Farsi, there was a demand that the song be translated into the English language so it could enjoy a greater reach among the people. Iranian-American singer, Rana Mansour, composed a popular version in English on You Tube, entitling it, "Woman, Life, Liberty."

Here is the English version of "Baraye," (For) a powerful ballad that has captured the hearts of millions of people, putting on display the desperate cries of the Iranian people struggling for freedom from a dictatorship government and yearning for a better life.

*Update: On February 5, 2023, Shervin's composition won a Grammy award for best song in "the social change" category. Shervin has put a face on the plight of all Iranians with his anthem song!

****

For dancing in the allies and the streets
For the thrill and the fear of getting caught kissing
For my sister, my brother, and unity
For all the times we tried to change their minds and stale beliefs
For the loss of pride, for poverty
For the dream of just a normal life for you and me
For all the children who are starving for a loaf of bread
For the greed of politics and all the lies they spread
For all the mass-polluted air we breathe
For all the litter in the streets and all the dying trees
For all the animals who suffer from elimination
For all the cats and dogs who love us without no conditions
For all the tears that seem to never end
For all the images that keep on turning in our heads
For a simple smile, to last a little while
For the future generations fighting for their time
For empty promises of heaven in the after-life
For all the imprisonment of beautiful minds
For all the babies who are born and for the ones who died
For all the times you told the truth, and all the times you lied
For all the speeches that we heard about a million times
For all the shacks and shelters that were sold to make a dime
For just a glimpse of a peaceful life
For the rising of the sun after an endless night
For all the pills we pop just to get some sleep
For all mankind, and our country
For all the boys and girls who never knew equality
For woman, for life, liberty
For liberty
For liberty
For liberty

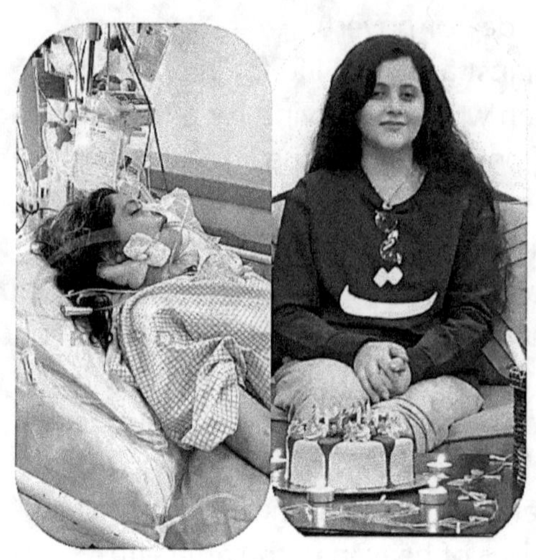

Dear Mahsa:
You courageously defied the Hijab Law.
Your unjust death sparked a revolution, an uprising that will never die!
"We are all Mahsa."

"They will not force us.
They will stop degrading us.
They will not control us.
And we will be victorious."
(Muse from their cd, "Uprising.")

<u>*Randy, please be our voice. They're killing us*</u>

I was relaxing in the break room at Chick Fil A just a few minutes before the beginning of my shift, when I received a voice message on Telegram. I noticed it was from my Iranian friend, Mahdis whom I hadn't heard from in a very long time. I immediately opened it up to listen to the message and was completely unprepared for what I was about to hear. In a trembling voice racked with tears and desperation, Mahdis pleaded with me from the other side of the world:

"Randy. Please be our voice. They're killing us! They're killing both young and old. Please be our voice!"

Chills ran up and down my spine. Tears filled my eyes. I was gripped by an intense feeling of urgency. I banged my fist down on the table in frustration. The lives of my Iranian friends were in danger and I wanted to be there right now to stand by their side and fight with them! For the last ten days, brave young women joined by men, in more than 110 cities across Iran, had taken to the streets, outraged over the senseless and brutal death of Mahsa Amini. The Morality Police had arrested her on September 13 for not wearing her hijab properly and showing too much hair. They explained to her brother that she was being transported to a detention center in Tehran to be re-educated on the Islamic dress code. A few hours later she was pronounced "brain dead" at a hospital, lapsing into a coma. The official explanation was that Mahsa had suffered a heart attack, but bystanders had witnessed her being beaten in the head as she was being forced into a police van.

The cruel and unjust death of Mahsa Amini had sparked a revolution with thousands of Iranian men and women taking to the streets outraged and demanding freedom from a dictatorship government. I had been very busy on my Facebook page, posting stories and videos in support for my dear Iranian friends. I had also reported on their plight and struggles for freedom on my blog talk radio program, "The Cross in the Desert." I immediately sent back a voice message assuring Mahdis that I would be her voice and the voice of all Iranians. I pleaded with her to be careful and told her that I would be praying for her safety.

"Randy, please be our voice."

I cannot adequately express into words, the awesome responsibility of being their voice. It is the passion and the driving force of my everyday life. It is the reason that I write their stories in my self-published books. I will never forget the incredible story that Mahdis shared with me a few years earlier right before the Persian New Year in Iran. She recalled a frightening incident one day at school when she was just a little girl. The teacher had sternly warned all the girls in the class that they had better wear their hijabs according to Islamic law or if not, that on judgment day, *"Allah would dangle them over the fires of hell by their hair!"*

Growing up in Iran, as a child, this was the picture of God that Mahdis had been taught. God was not a god of mercy or love, but rather a god of fear and retribution that could not wait to punish his disobedient children. You could hear in her trembling voice, that same little girl, now terrified and pleading with me to support them.

I bowed my head in prayer for Mahdis and remembered the awful story that I had read the day before about the tragic death of another young Iranian girl. Sixteen-year-old, Nika Shakarami, had bravely joined the protest in the streets and never returned home. Ten days later, her parents were told to come and see her lifeless body in the morgue. Nika's nose had been smashed in and her skull crushed. A few days earlier, twenty-two-year old Hadis Najafi is seen on a video tying back her blonde hair in protest and marching down the streets of Karaj only to be shot six times and killed for the crime

of wanting freedom. As I remembered these horrifying stories, I was gripped with the fear of that same tragedy happening to my dear friend Mahdis.
I could not bear the thought of that tragedy for another second, so I reluctantly got up from the chair to begin my job.

There is nothing more important to me in my life than being a voice for my Iranian friends. I'm not doing this for money, fame, or popularity. I do it because I love them. I do it because the Bible admonishes me to be their voice for freedom.

"Open your mouth for the mute, for the rights of all who are unfortunate and defenseless. Open your mouth, judge righteously and administer justice for the afflicted and needy."

(Proverbs 31:8-9)

Being silent in the face of injustice, cruelty, and the slaughter of human life, is an egregious sin that lacks any sense of humanity or compassion. It was the great German pastor, Dietrich Bonhoeffer, who courageously defended the church during World War II and was unafraid to stand up against Hitler. He rebuked the weak and afraid, proclaiming,

"Silence in the face of evil is itself evil: God will not hold us guiltless. Not to speak is to speak. Not to act is to act."

If Bonhoeffer were still alive today, I believe he would raise an accusing voice toward the mainstream media for their silence and ignorance when it comes to the human rights of the Iranian people. They are willingly silent in the face of evil! We need a prophetic voice that will be unafraid to confront the evil of silence and to confront the self-centered governments of this world who have economic ties with the Islamic Republic of Iran, lining their pockets with profits while ignoring their desperate cries. The Biden Administration is a prime example of sinful appeasement for the sake of a legacy.

They are willing to sit down at the table across from this terrorist regime and renegotiate a nuclear deal instead of rebuking them for their oppressive policies against innocent people, and speaking up for human rights. President Biden wants to have a legacy behind his name, like Barak Obama did in 2015, when he gave billions of dollars of sanction relief money to the Iranian government that was spent on furthering terrorism in the Middle East.

I refuse to be silent in the face of evil. Right after work, I messaged Mahdis back on Telegram, promising her that I will never back down and never give up until she can walk down the streets of Tehran one day without fear under a new government of freedom and democracy.

I want you to hear the desperate voice of Mahdis with me! I want you to feel the fear, the panic, and frustration tearing at her soul. It is only when we together raise our voices and bring awareness and condemn the evil, that Iranians have any hope for a bright future, a new tomorrow, where the shackles and chains of a dictatorship are finally torn away from their hearts and minds.

Speak up for those that cannot speak for themselves. It is our humanitarian duty. It is our calling.

Mahsa Amini
"A few strands of hair."

Jina Mahsa Amini peered out of the subway train window of the Tehran Metro. Tonight, the Tehran Metro was running right on schedule and would be arriving at *Haghani Station* within the next 5 minutes. It had been an extremely long travel day for her and her brother Ashkan. They had journeyed over 627 kilometers (389 miles) from the city of Saqqez, located in the Kurdistan Province near the border of Iraq.

Tonight, Jina was very excited! She was going to finally get to see her uncle for the first time in over a year. She quietly chuckled to herself, remembering back to when she was a child, he had proudly given her the nickname of "schne" meaning *gentle breeze*. Everyone in her family, including her friends, called her by her Kurdish name, Jina. Her Persian name, *Mahsa,* was reserved only for her passport, since Kurdish names were not accepted on official documents.

Jina reclined back in her seat and relaxed, closing her eyes for a few moments. This past summer had been an incredible time in her life. She had applied for university in Iraq to study biology and recently opened her very own Boutique shop, calling it, *"Best Boutique."* Having her own small business had been her biggest dream in life, made possible by her dear father. "Best Boutique," featured colorful Kurdish clothing, and a wide variety of women's jewelry. In just eight days she would turn 23 on September 21 and was planning on having the biggest birthday celebration of her life!

The sudden jolt of the subway train coming to a halt, startled Jina. She quickly opened her eyes and stood up from her seat. They had finally arrived at Haghani Station. It was exactly 6:15 pm. Following close behind her brother, they exited the train and stood outside the station. The evening sky was illuminated with brilliant streaks of orange and yellow. It was officially sunset in Tehran.

As Jina and her brother began walking away from the station, a woman dressed in a long black chador, flanked by two security officers dressed in military-green uniforms, stopped them. The woman gazed carefully at Jina's loose-fitting headscarf and then scrutinized the tight trousers that she was wearing. She shook her head in disgust and gave her a scornful look. Jina knew right away that this must be the *Tehran Morality Police.*

"May I see both of your passports?" The woman asked with a sharp tone in her voice.

Jina reached into her purse and Ashkan removed his wallet from his back pants pocket. The woman carefully inspected Jina's passport with a look of disapproval when she discovered her Kurdish background. She returned the passport to Jina and then edged closer with a stern look on her face.

"You have an improper hijab, miss. Do you know that?"

The woman reached up and touched the few strands of hair that were protruding from her loose-fitting headscarf. Jina took a deep breath, struggling to relax. She could feel her heart beginning to race in her chest. Beads of sweat began to trickle down her face.

"I'm sorry, mam. I was not sure what the clothing standards were for Tehran-"

"They are the same everywhere," The woman rudely interrupted. "Your hijab should be completely covering your hair. No make up or nail polish. No skin showing and these trousers. This is not proper clothing for a Muslim woman."

"As my sister explained," Ashkan interrupted, "We were not sure of the clothing standards, here,"

The woman glanced back at the security officers, motioning for one of them to escort Jina toward the waiting patrol van.

"We are going to solve that problem once and for all, Miss Jina. We are going to take you to the detention center for a few hours and re-educate you on the wearing of proper Islamic clothing."

Jina edged closer toward her brother, nervously grabbing him by the arm for security.

"No. No! Please don't let them take me, Ashkan!" Jina protested in fear.

Ashkan tried to stand between Jina and the morality police, but the guard shoved him out of the way, tightly grabbing hold of Jina's arm and pulling her toward the van.

"Let go of me!" Jina screamed, resisting with all of her strength.

Ashkan tried to pull Jina away from the grip of the guard, but the woman stepped between them and gave him a fierce look.

"Stand aside, or you too will be arrested."

A crowd of people had gathered after hearing the frightened screams of Jina. A few of them were busy filming the scene on their cell phones.

"Here is the address of the Vozara Detention Center. You can get a cab to take you there. Jina will be reunited with you in just a few hours."

Ashkan quickly entered the address into his cell phone and then began looking for a taxi driver. The vacation of a lifetime had suddenly been transformed into a living nightmare and Ashkan felt helpless to solve their dilemma. But there was one thing for sure. This was his sister and he was determined to not let anything bad happen to her!

****

Jina was frightened. She was terrified. As the morality officer forcibly dragged her toward the van, she resisted, looking back toward her brother to get one last look.

"Don't let them do this to me, Ashkan!" Jina pleaded, screaming in desperation.

The officer continued to restrain her and pushed her through the door into the tiny white van.

"Sit there!" the officer yelled, pointing to a tiny space in the rear of the van between two other women.

Jina flopped down between the two other women, trembling with fear. One of the women put her arm around Jina, struggling to console and calm her down. The female security officer climbed into the driver's seat and quickly started the van.

"I promise. I promise to never dress that way again. Just please let me go," Jina pleaded, her voice cracking with emotion. The male security officer took an angry deep breath and pointed his baton toward Jina. His eyes were bulging wide in anger and he began shaking the baton at her face.

"Shut up! Shut up! I'm tired of listening to your complaining."
One of the women tightly held onto Jina and drew closer to her, whispering in her ear.

'Shhh. Shhh. Just relax. It will be over soon. They will let us go."

Jina tried to stop shaking, but all she could remember was seeing the expression of fear on her brother's face. All she could think about right now, was seeing her uncle and running into his arms that she remembered doing years ago as a little child. Images of the hopes and dreams of her future raced through her mind. Right now, Jina felt threatened as if her life was about to end. She wanted to escape from this nightmare! Her heart began racing in her chest. She struggled to breathe.

"Let me out of here! Let me out of here!" Jina screamed, standing up from her seat.

Immediately, the security officer stood up and struck Jina against the side of her head with his baton. Falling backwards against the other women, Jina shrieked in pain, grabbing the side of her head. Blood began gushing out onto the clothes of the other women. The van took a sharp right turn and the female driver shouted back at the officer who struck Jina.

"What is going on? What are you doing?"

One of the women quickly removed her hijab and wrapped it tightly around Jina's head to stop the bleeding. Jina began sobbing loudly, holding onto to the wound on the side of her head. The officer who struck Gina, took a deep breath and put the baton back in the compartment on his belt buckle.

"That will teach you to shut up!"

Jina was withering in pain, fading in and out of consciousness. She tried to sit up, but felt nauseated and faint. Her vision was blurred and for a few moments, she was unaware of her surroundings. The woman continued to hold her in her arms and tried to console her. The bleeding had finally stopped. Jina lifted her head up from the woman's lap. The van pulled into the front entrance of the Vozara Detention Center. The driver turned off the engine. One of the other officers slid open the side door of the van. Jina tried to stand up but fell back down. She was extremely dizzy. Her head was spinning.

"Let's try to walk together. I will help you," the young woman promised, helping Jina stand up.

Jina slowly rose to her feet and tried to steady her balance. Her whole body was trembling with fear. The other two women stepped down from the side door of the van outside of the detention center waiting patiently for Jina. Taking a nervous deep breath, Jina stood at the sliding door entrance of the van. She saw the other girls, urging her to climb down and join them.

"Come on! Move," The security guard yelled, standing directly behind Jina.

Jina froze in fear. She didn't want to leave the van. She was terrified. Suddenly she felt another sharp blow to the back of her head. She slumped forward, desperately clinging onto the panel of the sliding door. The two women rushed to her aid to keep her from falling forward. Jina screamed in pain as she fell into the arms of the women.

"Stop it! Stop it!" One of the women yelled toward the officer. "You're going to kill her!"

The officer adjusted his shirt collar, putting his baton back on his belt and gave a devious look toward the women.

"She's Kurdish. She's getting what she deserves."

The women carefully escorted Jina inside of the detention center, holding her up with their arms. Arriving at the front desk for processing, two other female officers gazed toward Jina, who could barely stand up on her feet. One of the officers' snickered and said to the other. "She's pretending to be sick so she won't have to go to jail."

They both burst into laughter. Suddenly, Jina collapsed onto the floor, falling out of the arms of the two women.

"Help! Help!" One of the women screamed out loud. "Get a doctor!"

****

Ashkan had finally arrived outside of the Vozara Detention Center. He quickly paid the taxi driver and waited patiently by the front door. He glanced down at his cell phone. It was 7:30 pm. He remembered that the Morality Police had told him that Jina would be detained for just two hours and then be released. He began pacing back and forth, frustrated, and impatient. Glancing back down at his cell phone to pass the time, the blaring sound of sirens and the arrival of an ambulance caught his attention. He watched two medics leap out of the ambulance and rush in through the front doors of the detention center. Ashkan froze in fear. He was unsure of what was happening and was desperate for answers. He rushed toward the front door to follow the medics and was immediately restrained by a police officer.

"Stop. You can't go in there!"

Ashkan tried to push the officer out of the way but was forcibly restrained.

"I told you. You can't go in there," the officer warned him with a fierce look on his face.

While one of the medics began performing CPR on Jina's lifeless body on the floor, the police commander ordered the security officers into an adjacent room and closed the door.

"You are to say nothing about what you witnessed this evening to anyone or to the media. Do you understand? The camera footage will show Jina collapsing on the floor after arriving. Unfortunately, she suffered a heart attack, a cardiac arrest and the doctors at the hospital will corroborate our story.

****

Amjad gazed down at the lifeless body of his daughter, hooked up to machines and monitors in the ICU Ward of Kasra Hospital. He gently stroked the strands of Jina's black hair with his trembling hand and bent down, whispering in her ear.

"Please wake up dear daughter. I love you," Amjad pleaded, his voice cracking with emotion.

He drew closer toward her face, hoping that she had somehow heard him, but her eyes remained tightly shut. Amjad reached down and gently grasped hold of Jina's hand. It felt cold, clammy, and unresponsive. His mind flashed back to the time when his daughter rushed into his waiting arms as a beautiful young child full of life and adventure. Now his precious child lay motionless, in a deep coma, fighting for her life. Her still couldn't believe what Dr. Najafi had told him. *Jina was brain dead.* The resuscitation efforts had taken too long and vital organs had been compromised lacking sufficient oxygen.

With tears streaming down his face, Amjad gently kissed Jina on her forehead and caressed her hair.

"You were so full of life, dear daughter. You were so excited about your boutique shop and looked forward to attending university."

Amjad could feel the rage growing deep inside of his soul. The anger and frustration were tormenting him like a cancer. His whole body began shaking as he turned away from looking down at Jina. Struggling to restrain himself, he clenched his fist in anger. He refused to believe that his healthy daughter had suffered a heart attack and was now desperately clinging to life. He knew deep down in his soul that she had been the innocent victim of a brutal assault by an out-of-control morality policeman.

Taking a deep breath, Amjad turned away from the anger tormenting his soul and once again focused back on Jina, gently stroking her strands of hair with his trembling hand.

"Please wake up dear Jina. I just want to see your lovely brown eyes looking up at me. I just want to hear your sweet voice call me *Daddy.*"

The clicking sound of the door interrupted Amjad for a brief moment. He looked back and saw Dr. Najafi entering the room.

"I want to speak with you," Amjad insisted as he quickly moved away from Jina's bed. Dr, Najafi had a troubled look on his face as he moved to the side and held the door open for Amjad. They both went out in the corridor together. Ashkan was sitting in a chair, looking intently at his cell phone in the waiting room. He quickly stood up after seeing his father emerge out of Jina's room followed by the doctor.

Dr. Najafi took a deep breath and looked intently into Amjad's eyes.

"I wish I had better news about your daughter, Mr. Amini. I understand your fears and frustration. Unfortunately-."

"I don't want to hear it again," Amjad interrupted with a fierce look of anger in his eyes. "Do not tell me that my daughter suffered a heart attack. She was beaten. I know it!" Amjad proclaimed, pointing his finger toward the doctor's face."

Dr. Najafi gazed around the waiting room, seeing the troubled expressions on peoples' faces. He wanted to avoid a scene and struggled to calm Mr. Amini down.

"I want to see the CT scans of Jina's head now. They will prove that she was beaten!" Amjad insisted.

Ashkan got in between the doctor and his father and held up his cellphone.

"Look, Dr, Najafi. This is a video that the morality police posted on the internet. They are trying to prove that Jina fainted at the detention center, that she suffered from a heart attack. But its's false. It's obviously been edited!"

Dr. Najafi raised his hand up to calm Ashkan down. He nervously looked around the waiting room. People were staring intently at their conversation and getting very restless. He motioned toward a security officer stationed outside of Jina's room. The guard quickly approached them.

"I understand your anger, sir, but all I can say is that your daughter suffered a cardiac arrest from a pre-existing medical condition. She was not beaten- "

"You are lying, doctor. I know why. The police have instructed you on what to say and you're following their narrative."

"Mr. Amini," the security officer interrupted, "You must calm down or I will be forced to remove you."

Amjad covered his mouth with his hands in frustration. Tears streamed down his face. Ashkan put his arm around his father. Amjad quickly composed himself and gave an angry look toward the security officer.

"There are witnesses who told me that she was beaten. You know what I'm saying is true," Amjad shouted.

Ashkan pulled back on Amjad's arm, struggling to restrain him. Another security officer rushed over to take charge of the situation.

"You will be arrested if you don't calm down," the security officer warned Amjad.

Suddenly the sound of alarms interrupted their dispute. Dr. Najafi noticed a team of physicians rushing into Jina's room. Dr. Najafi excused himself and quickly joined them. Amjad burst into tears with Ashkan holding him tightly in his arms. The trauma had finally come to an end.

****

Amjad locked the front door of the boutique store for the last time. The boutique store had been the thrill and the lifelong dream of Jina's life. But now there would be no more clothing and jewelry sales. There would be no more unpacking of boxes and watching his daughter proudly display the latest fashions. Jina had been brutally murdered for simply allowing a few strands of hair to protrude out from underneath her hijab. Amjad was severely warned against talking to the media, but he didn't care. He refused to allow a dictatorship government to tell him what to say or what to do. A reporter had requested an interview with him today and he had taken him on a brief tour of the boutique shop. But now the lights had been turned off and the door had been locked for the very last time.

"You mentioned a special saying that had been written on Jina's gravestone," the reporter inquired.

Amjad's face beamed with joy as he remembered his last trip to her grave.

"Yes. It was my wife's idea and a very good one. It is two very powerful sentences and please do not forget to print this in your story. The gravestone says, *"Dear Jina. You won't die. Your name will become a symbol."*

After Jina's death, protesters removed their hijabs in defiance of the law and burned their headscarves in 146 cities across Iran yelling, "Death to the dictator." The government immediately shutdown the internet as they did in 2019, when over 1500 peaceful protesters were executed in the streets by the IRGC. In the first ten days, the uprising for freedom had been very costly with over 180 slain and 8,000 arrested. Iranian women had reached their absolute limit with an oppressive government that for over 40 years had treated them like second class citizens because of their gender. A young innocent Kurdish girl with her whole life ahead of her had become the latest victim of a dictatorship government. She was now the symbol of an uprising that would never die down like the previous ones. It was the beginning of the end for The Islamic Republic of Iran. The cracks in the foundation were now spreading and very soon a bloodthirsty regime would crumble into pieces.

****

<u>*Reflection*</u>

It has been said that, *"beauty is in the eye of the beholder."* God created women as beautiful creatures in his spiritual image so that they could reflect his handiwork to the world. Their beauty was never intended to be hidden for religious purposes. The Bible proclaims in Psalm 139:14, *"I praise you because I am fearfully and wonderfully made."*

God knit us together in our mother's womb. He fashioned every detail of our being so that we can display it to the world. Jina was a beautiful woman and as a woman she had the right to display her beauty. It's only a false religious system that restricts beauty and hides it under a veil, so that a man will not be tempted. However, the God of the Bible declares that he doesn't judge by appearance. In 1 Samuel 16:7, God says, *"The Lord doesn't see things the way you see them. People judge by outward appearance, but the Lord looks at the heart."*

The Islamic Republic of Iran is obsessed with outward appearances resulting in man-made rules that control women's bodies and suppress their beauty. Yet, God declares that we must stop making rules and judgments based on outward appearance. He sees our hearts. He sees our inward beauty. Unfortunately, the government of Iran refused to listen to God and murdered Jina for showing a few strands of hair.

<u>What Iranian women are saying about the protests</u>

"The most important protest they are doing right now is taking off their scarves and burning them. This is a women's movement first of all, and men are supporting them in the backline."

****

"Every morning I wake up and think, is this actually happening? Women making bonfires with their veils?"

****

"What you're seeing today is not something that just happened. There's been a long history of women protesting and defying authority in Iran."

A brief history of the hijab in Iran

"What you're seeing today is not something that just happened. There's been a long history of women protesting and defying authority in Iran."

The brutal and unjust murder of Jina Mahsa Amini by the morality police has a long history behind it. In order to understand and put into context the oppressive treatment of women by the present Iranian government, it is necessary to take a brief historical survey of the evolution of the Hijab Law in Iran.

Tihara Qurrat al- 'Ayn was one of the first women to unveil, questioning the political and religious orthodoxy in Iran. Tihara was a poet and religious scholar for the Bahai faith. She was very outspoken against the restraints placed on women and during a Babi conference in 1848, she unveiled before a congregation of men during a lecture. Her opposition to the treatment of women and her involvement within the Bahai faith, landed her in prison in 1852.

"You can kill me as you like, but you cannot stop the emancipation of women," Tahira proclaimed realizing her death was imminent.

In August of that same year, Tahira was first woman to be executed on the grounds of "corruption on earth." She was strangled to death by her own veil, thrown in to a shallow well, and stoned to death at the age of 35.

****

The first real challenge to the conservative religious establishment in Iran came by *Reza Shah*, General of the Persian Cossack Brigade, and recognized as the first Shah of the House of Pahlavi. He introduced social, economic, and political reforms, replacing Islamic Law with modern Western laws. It was under his reign that Iran became a constitutional monarchy. Striking out against the establishment, Reza Shah banned Islamic clothing, separation of the sexes, and the mandatory veiling of women. In 1936, he implemented "Kashf-e-hijab," a reform that was aimed at weakening the conservative/traditional religious system. The law stated that if a women wore a veil in public, the police had the right to remove it. The Shah regarded the hijab as a sign of "backwardness" and went so far as compelling men to wear western costumes and hats. The religious establishment was outraged at the new reforms and declared that the unveiling of women was a mortal blow to their values and power.

In 1941, when Reza Shah went into exile, the ban eased, allowing women to return to their traditional ways of dressing.

The Shah's son, *Mohammed Reza Shah Pahlavi* was also greatly influenced by western culture. In 1963, he introduced a series of reforms, called, "The White Revolution." One of the laws implemented gave women the right to vote. Four years later in 1967, women were finally granted equal rights in a male-dominated society. The age for marriage was raised from 13 to 18 years of age. This also angered the religious establishment. The Ayatollah Khomeini, who had been exiled by the Shah, began preaching the concept of an "Islamic republic," through books and cassette tapes. His sermons and teachings began to take root in the conservative/religious establishment, causing uprisings, and demonstrations by thousands of people. Unable to cope with the growing protests, and death threats, like his father before him, the Shah and his family were forced into exile in January 1979. This immediately opened the way for the Ayatollah Khomeini to return from exile in Paris and on February 1, he was greeted by millions of supporters in Tehran to begin the Iranian revolution.

The Ayatollah immediately reversed all of the reform policies of the Pahlavi Dynasty. Beaches and sports became "sex-segregated." Women were no longer allowed to serve as judges and the Islamic Clothing Law was re-instituted.

On March 8, 1979, International Women's Day, tens of thousands of women marched into Tehran, protesting the veil law. Three thousand women gathered in Qom, the religious city and residence of Khomeini. The women boldly marched into the city without wearing their veils, chanting, *"We didn't' have a revolution to go backwards."* There were also 15,000 protesters who gathered at the Palace of Justice for a three-hour sit in, presenting a list of demands, including the right of choice to dress, equal civil rights with men, and no discrimination in the political, social, and economic arenas. However, the new Ayatollah refused to listen!

In July of 1981, The Hijab law was passed and veiling in public became mandatory. Two years later, The Islamic punishment law was instituted stating that if a woman was caught unveiled in public, she would be sentenced to 74 lashes. Every reform of freedom that had been instituted by the previous Shah, had been completely abolished by the Ayatollah Khomeini. The oppression of women had begun, and they would be ruled by Islamic law from the cradle to the grave.

Under the presidency of Ahmadinejad in 2005, the Morality Police was established, which would begin patrolling the streets searching for offenders of the Hijab Law. The Iranian government recently has upgraded their efforts to prosecute women violators by implementing new technology using facial recognition. Now women are receiving citations in the mail for hijab violations even though they have not had any physical contact with law enforcement. Iran's national identity database, which was built in 2015 by the Cyber Police, contains facial scans for national ID cards. This database is being used to identify and catch veil law breakers as they travel to shopping malls and peruse the streets of Tehran.

In August of 2022, President Ebrahim Raisi introduced additional hijab and chastity restrictions. Women who violated the law can now lose access to banks, public transportation, and other essential government services. Repeat offenders can spend years in prison for refusing to veil publicly. This new technology is a policy shift that relies less and less on informants and physical contact with Morality Police. Digital surveillance had become the new tactic to keep track of "veil violators." The government is using their new technology to enforce their gender apartheid. In 2020, women began receiving text messages in their car, reminding them to wear a veil or be arrested. The facial recognition technology reduces the presence of police, especially cutting down on the brutal clashes between citizens, as in the case of Mahsa Amini. Facial recognition technology comes directly from the Chinese camera and artificial intelligence company, known as Tandy, Tandy is one of the largest security camera manufacturers in the world.

For over 43 years, the women of Iran have suffered greatly under a government dedicated to oppressing their human rights. From the ban on attending sports events to riding bicycles, women have reached their limit. They are rising from the ashes of discrimination. This is now their revolution!

"They may take our lives, but they'll never take our freedom!"
(William Wallace, from "Braveheart")

Hadis Najafi
"Preparing for battle"

Hadis Najafi ended her shift at the Takata Fast Food Restaurant at 5 pm and clocked out. It had been a very busy afternoon for the lead cashier in one of the most popular cafes in the city of Karaj. The city of Karaj lay nestled up against the majestic foothills of the Alborz mountain range, a distance of just six miles from the capital city of Tehran. Karaj city was a haven for young students studying art and medical science at Azad University. For Hadis, being a student was not her passion in life. Instead she was a dedicated "social media geek." She loved to display the latest fashions on her Instagram account and treat her fans to Persian dancing on Tik Tok. Politics and religion didn't interest her. She spent her money investing in VPN, to overcome the filtering of the internet, so she could talk to her friends online every night. The Islamic Republic of Iran along with the help of the cyber police had blocked the major social media platforms, Facebook, Twitter, Telegram, You tube, etc. The only way to overcome the government censorship was to purchase the virtual private network app.

As Hadis left the restaurant and stepped out onto the sidewalk, she looked carefully in both directions, to see if she could spot the

Morality Police Van and then ripped off her hijab and threw it down on the ground.

"I hate that damn thing!" Hadis muttered to herself.

This evening, Hadis was not her cheerful self. She was not in a good mood. The tragic death of Mahsa Amini had tormented her mind all day. Dealing with impatient customers paying for their meals and complaining about the prices had pushed her to the limit. She wasn't in the mood to listen to them, especially when a young Kurdish girl had been beaten to death by the Morality Police. Hadis had never been outspoken or political, but tonight was different. Every time she gazed at the picture of Jina Mahsa on her cell phone, lying comatose in a hospital bed, she couldn't hold back the tears. Deep down in her soul, she felt an irresistible urgency to see justice for Jina. Hadis felt it was her duty to humanity to be Jina's voice and scream loudly against the government 's unjust murder of an innocent young woman.

Hadis arrived at the bus stop and broke away from the crowd of people for a few moments. She quickly speed-dialed her friend Farzad.

"Dorood, Farzad (Faris for hi) Chetori?" (Farsi for, "How are you?")
"I'm good. You just get off work, Hadis?"
"Yes. I'm on my way home. Listen, I wanted to tell you. I am going to join the protest tonight. I heard they will be out on Eram Boulevard."

"Hadis, are you crazy? You've never been political."
"I know. I know," Hadis replied, stepping onto the arriving bus, "But I must do this for Jina. I believe we must be her voice. Women have got to rise and let this damn government know that we will not be oppressed anymore. We have the right to wear what we want to wear!"

"Please be careful, dear friend," Farzad cautioned Hadis.

Hadis clicked off her cell phone and relaxed back in her seat, taking a deep breath. Tonight, was Wednesday, September 21. Wednesday was her usual night for doing live Persian dancing for her fans on Tik Tok, but that would have to be postponed. She would celebrate with her fans later, but tonight was reserved exclusively for Jina. "Justice for Jina" was weighing heavily on Hadis's mind, and nothing was going to stop her!

****

Hadis walked through the front door of her home, exhausted, but energized to go back out. She decided to change her clothes and grab a quick bite to eat before joining the protest. As soon as she entered the kitchen, her mother noticed her flowing blonde hair draping down over her shoulders and a frustrated look in her brown eyes.

"Where is your hijab, Hadis? Didn't you wear it today? You must be so careful now these days."
Hadis flopped down in a chair at the kitchen table and grabbed an apple to eat.

"I threw that damn thing away. I hate it!" Hadis answered back while munching on her apple.

Mrs. Najafi sat down at the table across from Hadis with a worried look on her face.

"Hadis! Don't say that! You worry me! Look what happened to that Kurdish girl just last week!"

Hadis set the apple down in front of her and stared back intently at her mother.

"That's why I threw my hijab away, mom. I did it for Jina. I did it for every Iranian girl. We are tired of being oppressed and told what to do!" Hadis shouted back, banging her fist on the table.

Mrs. Najafi sat quietly and took a nervous deep breath. There was no arguing with her daughter. She was very high-spirited and independent. Hadis quickly stood up from the table and dabbed her lips with a napkin.

"I must go out tonight, dear mother. There is going to be a protest on Eram Boulevard. I need to go for Jina."

Mrs. Najafi rubbed her hand across her forehead and bowed her head in fear for a few moments. Then she stood up and hugged Hadis.

"I understand Hadis. But I am so worried. I am so afraid. It is so dangerous."

Hadis gave her mother a reassuring look and kissed her softly on the forehead.

"I must do this, mom. I will be careful. I promise I won't stay out very long."

Hadis left the kitchen and hurried into her bedroom. She quickly changed into a pink tank top and put on a fresh pair of blue jeans. She flopped across her bed and turned on her cell phone. The first picture that appeared was that of Jina Mahsa Amini, sitting in her living room last year, in front of a chocolate cake, celebrating her 22nd birthday. Hadis smiled. It was one of the happier moments for Jina. Hadis was also 22 years old, just like her hero, who was cruelly murdered just a week before her 23rd birthday. Tears filled her eyes. She blew a kiss toward the picture on her cell phone screen.

"Tonight, I will be your voice, dear Jina and I won't stop shouting until you get justice!"

****

"Death to the dictator! Woman, life freedom!"

The angry loud shouts of protesters filled the cool night air on Eram Boulevard. It was just a few minutes before 8 pm as Hadis turned on her cell phone. She aimed the camera toward the protesters filling the streets. Just up ahead she noticed a bonfire in the center of the street and watched several women setting their headscarves on fire. Running swiftly toward the scene, Hadis began narrating the live video she was creating for her friends.

"This is a scene of women burning their hijabs," Hadis shouted out loud in laughter. "You go girls!"

In the distance she heard sirens and more angry shouts of protesters chanting. Tonight, she felt energized and unafraid. She had never been to a protest before. Hadis remembered back to 2019 when more than 1500 peaceful protesters were gunned down in the streets. At that time, she vowed to never be political and just mind her own business. But all of that suddenly changed with the death of Jina. Tonight, was personal. Tonight, she had to make a stand for the women of Iran. She regretted her decision for being so selfish and passive a few years ago, but that had all changed.

Passing a local hardware store, Hadis paused, catching her breath, spoke directly into her cellphone continuing to film the protest.

"I hope in a few years, when I look back, I will be happy that things have changed for the better. I like to think that, when I look back at this a few years later, I'll be pleased that I joined the protest."

A few women, following close behind her, began chanting, "Woman, life, freedom." They were carrying signs with a picture of JIna Mahsa Amini. At the bottom of the sign, it read, *"We are all Mahsa."* Hadis was excited to see that that two young men were in the crowd of women chanting along with them. It was so encouraging for her to see men involved in the uprising and defending the rights of women.

Suddenly, the sounds of security forces yelling for protesters to halt or they would shoot, startled Hadis. Beads of sweat began rolling down her face. She took an angry deep breath and vowed once again to not be afraid. Putting her cell phone in her pants pocket, Hadis stood still for a moment. She tied back her blonde hair into a ponytail and twisted a rubber band around it to hold it into place. An exhilarating feeling of courage surged through her body. Tying back her hair was like preparing for battle. Tonight, Hadis was making a bold statement to the government that she refused to comply with the man-centered Hijab Law. This was her hair, her body, and no man had the right to control it or tell her what to do.

The security forces began clashing with the protesters, beating some in the head with their batons. Instead of cowering in fear, Hadis closed her eyes and in her mind's eye, she remembered back to her favorite movie, "Braveheart." She could see the chilling scene, where William Wallace was laying across a torture rack and the King pleading with him to recant and beg for mercy. She smiled, remembering the famous last shout from William Wallace's lips, when he screamed, "Freedom!"

The first shot terrified Hadis! She clutched her abdomen in excruciating pain. A barrage of shots immediately followed the first one, sending frightened protesters scrambling for cover. Hadis collapsed backwards on the hard pavement, struck by five more bullets in the neck, chest, and face. The beautiful blonde freedom fighter lay dead on the street in a massive pool of blood. She had made her courageous last stand on Eram Boulevard in the city of Karaj, unafraid and unashamed to die as a martyr for freedom in the never-ending struggle against the gender apartheid in Iran.

****

A few days after her tragic death, a video surfaced showing a young woman tying back her blonde hair and preparing to join the protest in Karaj. The video was attributed to Hadis, just seconds before she was fatally shot. Although there is some controversy concerning the video being that of Hadis, nevertheless, it had been unanimously attributed to her as showing the final seconds of her life.

Security forces refused to hand over Hadis's body to her family at the hospital until they signed a pledge stating that she died of natural causes. Devastated over her tragic death, a family member, who was enlisted in the Basij (Iranian paramilitary) was finally granted permission to make a formal identification of the body. He verified that it was indeed Hadis and was horrified upon examination, that she suffered at least 20 gunshot wounds to her body at very close range.

Mrs. Najafi, even though being warned by security not to speak publicly about her daughter's death, declared, "My daughter was murdered for the hijab, for Mahsa Amini. She wanted to keep Masha's name alive. Mahsa is also my daughter and all those killed are my children. She died for Mahsa. She sacrificed herself for Mahsa."

Shortly after her death, Hadis's sisters, Afsoon and Shirin, published her photos and told people that she was shot, defying the government ban.

****

Reflection

Understanding the great risk, Hadis Najafi bravely took to the streets and proudly declared her right as a woman, to display her beauty, rejecting the mandatory Hijab Law. She died for the right to choose and the freedom to say no to a dictatorship government. In the last seconds of her life, she spoke up for Mahsa Amini and all Iranian woman, when she tied back her hair and faced the firing squad.

Jesus proclaimed in John 10:10:

"The thief does not come except to steal, and to kill, and to destroy. I have come that they may have life, and that they may have it more abundantly."

For more than 40 years, The Iranian people, especially women, have suffered greatly at the hands of a corrupt and controlling government. They have had their dignity stolen, their freedom suppressed, and their lives destroyed by satanic forces. Jesus is the Good Shepherd. He desires to gently lead and guide us. Satan desires as his core mission, to kill and destroy us. In contrast, Jesus promises to protect and provide for his people. His mission is to bring us life and life to the fullest. He came to bring you true hope and freedom. He promises to remove the shackles of your oppression and give you a life filled with meaning and purpose.

Nika Shakarami
Burning headscarves in Tehran

Nika tied her black hair back into a ponytail and gazed back down at her cell phone. She quickly texted her friend and promised to meet her in a few hours by Laleh Park. This evening, there was going to be a huge protest rally and Nika was determined to be a part of it. It had been four days since the death of Mahsa and Tehran had been transformed into a battlefield. Both men and women had converged on the streets, setting fire to police cars, throwing rocks at security officers, and burning their headscarves in defiance of the Hijab Law.

Nika had recently moved to Tehran from Khorramaabad in the Lorestan province to stay with her aunt after the death of her father. She was very close to her Aunt Atash. They had a strong relationship and living with her gave her closer access to her sister's dormitory at university. Nasrin, Nika's mother, had no choice but let her go and live in Tehran. Ever since she was a little toddler, Nika made it very clear to her parents that she was a free spirit, an independent young lady with a mind of her own. In just twelve days, she would turn 17 and was already planning the birthday celebration of her life with her best friends.

"Woman, life, freedom!" The loud chants of protesters echoed from the speakers of her cell phone. Nika smiled and clenched her fist in support of the protest video. She wasn't afraid! The police didn't frighten her at all. What they did to Jina Mahsa was unacceptable. Her name, Nika, in Persian, literally meant, *victory, pure crystal water.* Tonight, Nika was determined to live up to the meaning of her name by fearlessly standing up to a dictatorship government and giving it a piece of her mind!

"Here is the bottled water and the towel that you wanted," Aunt Atash said, walking into her bedroom.

Nika quickly turned off her cell phone and stood up, trying to act causal. She didn't want her aunt to know anything about her activities later that evening.

"Merci, (Farsi for thank you) Aunt Atash," Nika replied, gently kissing her on her forehead.

Nika secured a black backpack around her shoulders that contained her ID card and took the towel and the bottle of water from her aunt's hand.

"Your sister will be very happy to see you," Aunt Atash said with a proud look in her eyes.

Nika smiled back and nervously bit her upper lip. She wasn't proud of lying to her aunt but she would never approve of her taking part in a protest. Aunt Atash was very overprotective of her niece. She knew how outspoken Nika was against the government oppression of women, but believed that the best course of action was to keep silent and stay safe. The idea of Nika being sent to prison would be too much for Atash to emotionally accept.

Therefore, Nika knew she had to conceal her activities. Tonight, was Tuesday, September 20, the fourth day in a row of the uprising. Tehran was slowly becoming a war zone and being out on the streets was very dangerous.

"I will not stay out late. I will see you in a few hours," Nika promised, giving Aunt Atash a tight hug.

"Behave yourself," Aunt Atash said with a chuckle and a twinkle in her eyes, realizing that Nika would totally ignore her wishes.

Nika once again hugged her aunt and laughed, "You don't need to worry, Aunt Atash. You know me!"

****

The streets adjacent to Laleh Park were swarming with loud, angry protesters chanting, "Woman, life, freedom!" Nika was pleased to see that several men were supporting their sisters in the protest and marching right alongside them shouting, "I will kill, I will kill those who killed my sister!"

The loud chanting of *"Azadi, azadi, azadi* (farsi for freedom) was music to Nika's ears. She quickly ran up to a group of protesters carrying signs, and yelled at the top of her lungs, "Azadi. Azadi. Azadi!" The sun was beginning to set on the massive crowd. It was 7:30 pm. In the middle of the street, Nika was thrilled to see women forming a circle and burning their hijabs, with cars honking their horns and shaking their fists at them for blocking traffic. Beyond the circle, Nika noticed a group of young men hurling stones at some Basij members riding on motorcycles and then racing toward the sidewalks. One Basij rider had abandoned his motorcycle and was pursuing a group of teenagers, waving his steel baton in the air.
In the center of the street, Nika noticed an overturned trash bin

and a small fire burning next to it. Leaping into action, Nika ran toward the trash bin and proudly stood on top of it, waving her hijab in the air, screaming "Death to the dictator!" Immediately a group of young teenagers surrounded her on the trash bin and began shaking their fists in the air, chanting, *"Death to Khamenei! Death to Khamenei!"* Right below the trash bin, a young girl pulled out her cell phone and pointed it toward Nika standing above her. She began recording the live event, describing it to her friends.

Nika pulled a black mask from out of her pants pocket and tied it across her face. She then reached down and took a burning cloth from the hand of a teenager and set her hijab on fire. She raised the scarf in the air above her head. The protesters below began clapping their hands in celebration.

"Woman, life, freedom!" Nika screamed at the top of her lungs, holding the burning scarf above her head. Then a few seconds later, she hurled the burning scarf down onto the street and jumped up and down in celebration.

The loud bangs of gunfire startled Nika and the protesters. She leaped down from off the trash bin. Security forces were descending on their protest, marching toward them in orderly files and firing tear gas pellets into the crowd. Nika grabbed her towel to shield her eyes, as a cloud of smoke surrounded them. This caused many protesters to flee, covering their faces and coughing.

"Stop now, or we will shoot you!" one of the police officers declared as he held a bull horn up to his mouth.

Nika followed two young teenagers as they ducked down behind a black car parked on the side of the street. The agonizing sound of young girls screaming caused her to cover her ears in fear. The security forces were using both live ammunition and pellets, firing at them from close range. Some of the young girls were struck in the eye with the pellets and fell to the ground, covering their face with their hands. Nika couldn't look. She turned away. The sound of rapid gunfire sent chills down her spine. Suddenly her cell phone began ringing. She looked at the screen and could see her mother's name appearing.

"I can't talk right now!" Nika nervously stuttered. Nasrin could hear the loud shouting and the sound of gunfire in the background.
"Please come home, right now Nika! I'm begging you!" Nasrin pleaded.

Nika looked up from the parked car. The security forces were getting closer. Basij members on their motorcycles were chasing after protesters, waving their batons in the air. She pushed the cell phone closer up against her ear, struggling to hear her mother's voice.

"Mom, I can't talk right now! I'll call you later!" Nika shouted and then hung up.

One of the teenagers stood up, shouting back at the security forces and began hurling rocks at them. There was a loud bang in response and he immediately fell back down behind the car, clutching his face. He had been shot in the eye with a pellet.

Nika grabbed the teenager and held him in his arms. She pulled out the towel from her pocket to try and stop the bleeding from his eye.

"We cannot go the hospital," the other teenager cried out with fear in his voice, "They will find us there."

Nika helped the teenager to his feet and they began running, dodging the tear gas pellets, and keeping close to the sidewalk. In a few blocks, they would reach Keshavarz street, and hopefully find safety away from the security forces. As they rounded the corner, the teenager, out of breath, and suffering with great pain, told them to leave him and urged them to quickly escape. Nika reluctantly left the young boy sitting on the sidewalk. She gave him her towel and quickly caught up with the crowd of other protesters fleeing the scene. Night had fallen in Tehran, as they ran in and out of traffic on Keshavarz Boulevard, struggling to avoid detection from security forces. The sound of sirens and flashing lights, forced the group to swiftly run the opposite way. Security officers, their face covered with shields and dressed in riot gear, began descending on the crowd of protesters, beating women in the heads with their batons. The crowd that Nika was running with had suddenly disbanded and she found herself all alone and frightened.

Ducking down for cover behind a white car, stranded in traffic in the middle of Keshavarz Boulevard, Nika pulled out her cell phone to call her friend Sahar.

"Sahar. This is Nika. I'm being chased by security forces. I'm hiding behind a car-"

The call was disconnected. Sahar could no longer hear Nika's voice.

Nika felt the strong aggresive hands of two police officers, forcibly grabbing her and lifting her up from the pavement behind the stalled car. She tried to fight back, yelling, and cursing at them, but was instantly subdued by the painful strike of a steel baton against the back of her head. She fell backwards out of their arms and collapsed in pain as they dragged her toward the open doors of a waiting van.

****

Nika had been apprehended by the IRGC (Iran Revolutionary Guard Corps.) and was swiftly transported to an interrogation room at their headquarters. She leaned forward in her chair with both of her hands pressed up against her head, writhing in pain from being struck by the baton of a policeman. There were two guards stationed next to the front door and a tall, heavyset, bearded man pacing the floor in front of the table of the dimly lit room. The interrogator stopped pacing for a moment to light up a cigarette. He took a long puff and then began pacing again. The hypnotic tapping sound from his steel boots was annoying to Nika as she sat silently with her head bowed down between her hands. The interrogator stopped once again and then pressed both of his hands down on the table and stared intently toward Nika.

"You are a whore, a prostitute, burning your hijab in public," he screamed toward Nika.

Nika turned her face away from the interrogator and refused to make eye contact with him. The interrogator took an angry deep breath and another long puff on his cigarette. Then without warning, he pressed his cigarette up against Nika's arm to tantalize her. Nika recoiled and pressed her chair up against the wall, refusing to give into his tactics. The interrogator's face grew red with anger. He tossed his cigarette down on the floor and quickly crushed it with the heel of his boots. There was a long silence. Nika kept facing toward the wall.

Suddenly, the interrogator grabbed her by the arm. Her chair scooted back toward the table as Nika struggled to stay seated. The interrogator grabbed onto her hair. Nika tried to resist, but was forced to look him squarely in the face. She could see the deep hatred in his black eyes and feel the hot presence of his breath on her face. She began trembling with fear and struggled to turn her face away from him.

"You can make this easy for the both of us," The interrogator said in a calm voice. He snapped his finger and one of the guards quickly responded laying a white piece of paper on the table in front of Nika. The interrogator laid a black pen down next to the piece of paper and gazed intently toward her once again.

"If you sign this piece of paper, confessing that you were wrong to protest and burn your hijab and then agree to be videotaped here in this room, promising to never protest again and comply with the hijab law, you will be released today."

The interrogator waited patiently for a response from Nika, but Nika turned her back on him and stared toward the wall. Nika's silence infuriated the interrogator. He lifted his arms up from the table and quickly lit up another cigarette. He began pacing back and forth in front of the table like a hungry vulture waiting to kill its prey. Then he abruptly stopped, staring intently at Nika with his black piercing eyes. Nika remained silent with her back turned away from him.

"I know that you have an Instagram and Telegram account. I know you are posting protest videos on these accounts. Now you will tell me your passwords, right now. Give them to me!" The interrogator demanded.

Nika remained silent, refusing to look her interrogator in his eyes. The interrogator took an angry deep breath and began pacing again. The hypnotic sound of his boot heels echoing against the floor continued to annoy Nika, but she remained silent, refusing to answer his questions. He stopped pacing once again and then lunged forward toward Nika. He grabbed her by the hair again. Nika resisted and pulled away from his grip. However, he succeeded in forcing her to look him in the eyes.

"If you don't tell me right now, I will kill both your mother and your aunt!"

Nika bit her bottom lip and began trembling. She stared back at her interrogator with a fierce, non-compliant look in her eyes and then spit directly into his face. Stunned by her vindictive response, the interrogator quickly wiped the spit from his face and then reached back behind his belt. He lifted his steel baton in the air and then repeatedly struck Nika in the head with his eyes bulging in anger. Nika fell out of her chair, onto the floor trying to shield the blow with her arms. The interrogator continued bashing in Nika's head with his baton without stopping or pausing. Streams of blood splattered up against the wall as the two guards silently watched on in horror. Finally, the interrogator stood back up and wiped off the bloody baton with his handkerchief. Nika's lifeless body laid sprawled across the floor next to the table. The brave freedom warrior had drawn her last breath in the struggle against a brutal and oppressive government. She had lived up to her name. Nika was victorious. In the last hours of her life, she had courageously defied a dictatorship government and shed her blood for the freedom of her people.

****

On the morning of September 21, Nika's aunt and mother filed a missing person's report when she failed to return home. They searched Gharchak and Evin prisons, police stations, and detention centers, asking for a list of who had been arrested. Finally, after nine agonizing days, they were summoned to Kahrizak prison to identify her body. They had only allowed them to see Nika's face and observed that her nose had been smashed.

Horrified and grief-stricken, Nika's family demanded to know what happened to her. Security forces explained that her death was not the result of the protests but a fall from a building. They showed video footage to Nika's mother of a young girl, purported to look like Nika, entering a building, and then minutes later hitting the pavement below, the result of a fall. Nasrin denied that the girl in the footage was her daughter and claimed that the picture of her lying on the pavement below, looked staged. Later they would claim that Nika committed suicide. Trying to hide their lies and deceit, the government forced family members to make a false confession on State TV that Nika didn't participate in the protests, but died as a result from an "accidental" fall from a building.

The night before her burial, Nika's mother had a closer look at her body and noticed the mark of an incision across her stomach. She was informed that the incision was the result of an autopsy, but she disputed that explanation, believing that Nika's organs had been removed and sold on the black market. A few days later, Nasrin, Nika's mother, was presented with a death certificate that completely contradicted the story put forth by the regime. The death certificate showed that Nika died as a result of *"multiple blows to the back of her head."*

The next day, October 2, which would have been Nika's 17th birthday, her body was secretly stolen by government agents and buried at a remote village in order to discourage any large crowds of demonstrations. With tears streaming down her face, Nasrin proclaimed, *"It was your birthday today my love. Today, I must congratulate you on your martyrdom."*

Reflection

The government deliberately covered up the death of Nika and engaged in painful deception to hide the truth from her family. They allowed them to suffer for nine days in a desperate search for their daughter, knowing all the time what had happened to her.

The Bible declares in Ecclesiastes 12:14,
"God will judge everything we do, including every secret thing, whether good or bad."

Jesus proclaimed in Luke 12:2-3,
"For there is nothing covered that will not be revealed, nor hidden that will not be known. Therefore, whatever you have spoken in the dark will be heard in the light, and what you have spoken in the ear in inner rooms will be proclaimed on the housetops."

God is a holy God. He will hold this government accountable for Nika's unjust death. Their lies will be exposed and the truth will be revealed. The wicked believe that their evil deeds will remain secret but the Bible proclaims that every lie will be exposed by the glorious light of God's truth. Nika bravely stood up against an oppressive government and was brutally executed for the crime of wanting freedom. Her blood will be avenged!

Asra Panahi
"I refuse to sing."

I can distinctly remember a few years ago during the racial unrest in America, that a select number of players of the NFL, refused to stand during the singing of the National Anthem, and instead kneeled. They were convinced that the "cancer of racism" in America had deeply infected every institution and that African-Americans had been wrongly targeted by police officers. In order to make their convictions known and their voices heard, they decided to take a knee during one of the most sacred moments in a sporting event.

Their act of protest deeply offended many Americans, including myself, who felt that the timing of their protest was an insult to the brave men and women of the military who put themselves in harms way to defend our freedoms. While I respected their right to protest and exercise their first amendment rights, I thought that the occasion of their protest was very wrong. The American flag and the heroes who fought for it, guarantees our freedom of speech, our freedom to assemble, and our freedom of religion. The national anthem is a solemn reminder that freedom is not really free, and many brave Americans had shed their blood to protect that all important, seven-lettered-word called, *"Freedom."*

However, in the heat of the moment, when my blood pressure was soaring and my heart was filled with rage, I remembered the famous quote from the French philosopher Voltaire, who declared, "I may not agree with what you have to say, *but I will defend to the death your right to say it."*

The famous quote from Voltaire puts everything into perspective. It's true, I really hate the things some people say and it really offends me, but our constitution guarantees them the right to say it, and I must heed the words of Voltaire and afford them the right to say whatever is on their minds, regardless of how it offends me!

Thousands of miles away in the tiny Iranian city of Ardabil, a lesser known athlete was making her mark on the sport of swimming. Fifteen-year-old, Asra Panahi was recognized as the top swimmer in the East Azerbaijan Province of Iran. She had won the bronze (third place) in the 50m and 100m freestyle during the individual competition at the tender age of 12, and now three years later, she had made a name for herself. However, it wasn't swimming that catapulted her to gain worldwide recognition this time. Instead, it was Asra's refusal to sing.

The students at Shahed Girls School in Ardabil had been bused to a special event, a pro-government rally where they were forced to sing a song praising the Supreme Leader of Iran. The event took place on October 12, just three weeks after the unjust death of Jina Mahsa Amimi. The young girls were in no mood to sing. They refused to raise their voices, and one of those voices was that of Asra Panahi. The avid swimmer joined the rest of her schoolmates and remained silent. Instead, they all chanted, "death to the dictator."

Once they returned to the school, the principal, outraged at their "non participation" in singing the pro-government song, summoned security forces. When the security forces arrived, they immediately began beating the young school girls, arresting ten of them. Twelve other young girls were rushed to the hospital suffering from trauma to their heads, one of them being Asra Panahi. Three days later, the famed swimmer of Iran, succumbed to her injuries, and died.

When I read about Asra's death, I wept. Asra was an athlete just like the famous football players of the NFL. She didn't have the name recognition that they had, but as a human being, she had the same right to say no. Asra had the right to refuse to sing, just like the football players. However, her right was not respected. Her right was denied with a swift blow to the head by a police officer carrying out his duty under the orders of a dictatorship government. Asra was outraged by the treatment of women in Iran, and she refused to raise her voice to an oppressive leader. Her refusal was met with violence and death. Her rights were swiftly denied as a reminder to all other schoolgirls that obedience is not an option in the Islamic Republic of Iran.

The cruel and unjust death of Asra Panahi is a painful reminder that we still take our freedoms way too much for granted. It is truly sad to think that one day soon, Asra may have won the gold medal in swimming at the Olympics. She may have attained world-wide name recognition as some American athletes, but we will never know that for a fact. Her voice was silenced by a cruel government who refused her right not to sing.

On October 12, 2022, a young Iranian swimmer won my heart forever. She exceeded in winning a gold medal in swimming. She made her mark on humanity with an act of courage heard round the world. Asra refused to honor a dictator. She refused to sing for a murderer. She spoke up boldly for all Iranian women and the rest of the women of the world. We must never forget her supreme act of bravery. Asra defines exactly what the word freedom truly means!

<u>Psalm 10/The Passion Translation</u>
"God promises to put an end to the oppression of the wicked."

Psalm 10 echoes the desperate cries of my heart for my Iranian friends. It is a plea for God to put an end to the oppression of the wicked. I am overwhelmed so many times by the inhumane evil that is done to Iranian men and women. I cry out to God for justice and relief to their suffering. Where are you God? Why are you silent? Why do you allow the wicked to prosperous and the righteous to suffer? As you read this psalm of lament, make it personal. Let it be the cry of your heart for God to finally put an end to the unjust suffering of the Iranian people.

Lord, why do you seem so far away when evil is near?

Why have you hidden yourself when I need you the most?
The arrogant in their elitist pride persecute the poor and helpless.
May you pour out upon them the very evil they've dreamed up against others! How they brag and boast of their cravings, exalting the greedy. They congratulate themselves as they despise you—these arrogant ones, so smug and secure! In their delusion the wicked boast, saying, "God doesn't care about what we do. There's nothing to worry about!" So successful are they in their schemes and prosperous in all their plans! Your laws are far from them; they scoff at their enemies. They boast that neither God nor

men will bring them down. They sneer at all their enemies, saying in their hearts, "We'll have success in all we do and never have to face trouble." Their mouths spew out cursing, lies, and threats. Only trouble and turmoil come from all their plans. Like beasts lurking in the shadows of the city, they crouch silently in ambush, waiting for the innocent to pass by. Pouncing on the poor, they catch them in their snare to murder their prey in secret as they plunder their helpless victims.

They crush the lowly as they fall beneath their brutal blows, watching their victims collapse in defeat! Then they say to themselves, "The Lofty One is not watching while we do this. He doesn't even care! We can get away with it!" Now arise, Yahweh-God! Crush them once and for all! Don't forget the helpless and oppressed. How dare the wicked think they'll reject God and escape judgment. They say to themselves, "God won't hold me accountable." Lord, I know you see all that they're doing, noting their each and every deed. You know the trouble and turmoil they've caused.

Now punish them thoroughly for all that they've done! The poor and helpless ones trust in you, Lord, for you are famous for being the helper of the fatherless. I know you won't let them down. Break the power of the wicked and all their strong-arm tactics. Search them out and destroy them for the evil things they've done. You, Yahweh, are King forever and ever! All the nations will perish from your land. Yahweh, you have heard the desires of the humble *and seen their hopes.* You will hear their cries and encourage their hearts. The orphans and the oppressed will be terrified no longer, for you will bring them justice, and no earth-dweller will trouble them again.

<u>Heather Joy</u>
"From ashes to beauty, a prophetic voice for Iranians."

I want to introduce you to a very special friend who also has a passion for the salvation and freedom of Iranians. Heather Joy is a Prophetic Bible teacher. God has given her a great love for the Iranian people and has used her painful past experiences to bring hope to them. Several years ago, Heather was the victim of sexual abuse and for many years struggled to find healing for her scars. In His perfect timing and wisdom, The Lord began the healing process and has used Heather's painful experiences for His glory. Heather has reached out to Iranian women who were also victims of rape to give them hope for their painful traumas.
This is her incredible story.

I pray that you are inspired by the courage expressed within these stories. Allow me to introduce myself and share my heart with you. My name is Heather. To give you some background, my story is one that was filled with darkness and cruelty but it is being transformed into one marked by redemption. Growing up, there was chaos in the home. My father did not readily enjoy our presence too often. He was often angry, sometimes without provocation. When my sister and I started attending school, she was always (and still is) the social butterfly in the family. When we were not in school, she was always with her friends. That was her escape. I was the opposite. I was a homebody. I often stayed in my room and did my homework or worked on various art projects. As a result, I often received the brunt of my father's wrath, especially before bedtime. I remember getting ready for bed and brushing my teeth. In the house we lived in, the bathroom was adjacent to my parents' bedroom. The sliding door was open for most of the time and after I finished getting ready for bed, he would forcefully grab my arm and throw me against the bed before hitting me with his hands or a belt nearby. My mother never knew the full scope of my father's wrath toward me until he walked out on our family when I was 11. My mother would face abuse from him in the form of word curses and other activities he did behind her back, while she worked to provide for the home and sought to create happy memories for our family.

School was not any easier. I was often bullied, all the way to my first semester in college. Kids would throw me in trash bins or down the stairs. I had been forcefully thrust against the bathroom stall or the wall as I was switching between my classes. I will never forget the time when I was beaten by multiple kids on the bus before we headed out to a soccer game. There were three girls and two of them unleashed their anger upon me while the third girl stood by. One of the girls took me by the hem of my shirt and thrust me against the window before punching me in the face and the torso repeatedly. Her friend then began to throw me down to the ground where they all joined in and kicked me repeatedly while they shouted insults at me. I managed to protect my face as they pummeled me and when they had finished, they began to saunter off the bus and head towards the field. I waited a minute or two before I rose to my feet. I did not say anything because I did not want to forfeit this game.

Two games prior to this one had been cancelled. I was a right forward and I loved the game, so I pushed through the pain and played until the next quarter. Sometimes, it felt like my mere existence made me a target for their hatred and hurtful words. Word curses became a common thing in my life and this would become much worse as I entered my teen years and into adulthood. I grew used to being alone in a social context, but I thrived as a team player in ministry or in the context of teaching or public speaking. As I began to hit my teen years, the bullying continued in high school so I kept to myself. I was more of a studious type so I enjoyed typing papers and working on projects. I also participated (and greatly enjoyed) taking part in our school theater program because it was the only time that the bullying ceased. Outside of my education, I was thrown into the trap of comparison. In relation to my sister and my cousins, I could never measure up and this feeling of unworthiness only increased as we all matured into adulthood.

Prophetically speaking, it was during my early teen years that I started having dreams and visions. When I was 13, I had two visions within the same day. It was the summer of 2003 and I had spent the entire day with a group of friends from church. The weather was perfect and the birds were chirping. We had started the day by going out to breakfast and then we caught an early matinee. After the movie, as we were driving, we stumbled upon the county fair. Of course, we had to go! We enjoyed all the yummy fair treats and rode on all the rides. We managed to leave the fair briefly for dinner before we returned to the fair until it closed. It was a lovely time of fellowship, and what better way to end the night, than to have a sleepover. We made it a point to stop at Walgreens. We grabbed some movies from Redbox and picked up some snacks inside. My friends had all separated, and as I stood in the candy aisle, I received my first vision. I saw in the Spirit, two cars colliding. I heard the sound of metal crunching against metal. Lights were flashing in the background. I came out of the Spirit, and the Lord with urgency, told me to WAIT. I needed to tell my friends to wait because something was about to happen. In hindsight, I realized that the Lord was calling me to the prophetic, but at the time, I was unaware of my spiritual giftings or my calling.

I did not heed the Lord's urgency in that moment, and as such, my friends did not receive the Lord's warning either. We had gathered what we thought we needed and paid for our items before exiting the store. As we reach the intersection, Boom! The vision that I had just received while I stood in the candy aisle had come true. Someone had hit our car from behind. The driver was so intoxicated that he kept going, not realizing that he had just crashed into another vehicle. He pushed us across the intersection and into the opposite lane on the left side. A second hit. The lights at the intersection had just turned green. Boom! We sustained a third hit from the left side. A couple seconds later, Boom! We sustained a final hit to the right side and my friend's car was smashed into the shape of a box. Witnesses saw the scene and called 911 on our behalf. It was labeled by paramedics as a DOA or dead-on arrival. There were 6 of us (including myself) and we all managed to crawl through the sun-roof. At that time, it was almost 11:30pm at night. We were in shock, to say the least, but knowing that we had survived such a deadly card accident unscathed, we were eternally grateful to be alive. Witnesses who saw the accident from start to finish began to join us in the turn lane while we waited for the police and the paramedics to arrive. Our gut instinct was to use that time and pray. One of the witnesses, a woman, was a Holy Spirit filled Christian, and she started our prayer circle.

We held hands, and as she prayed, I looked up. I received a second vision. Remember, it was 11:30 at night so it was pitch black. As I looked up, there was a glorious light. I looked briefly back into the natural realm where I saw cars zooming by and they had their headlights on, but when I looked back into the Spirit, this light was more glorious than I could ever describe. As I continued watching this scene in the Spirit, I saw chariots of angels and they made a perimeter. They were creating sound in the heavenlies and singing "Holy, Holy, Holy is the Lord God Almighty" repeatedly. I watched this scene for about 15 minutes, and when this woman finished praying, the vision was closed. The police questioned us, as if we ourselves were witnesses. They were shocked to find out that we were the victims at the scene of the accident but by God's grace and hedge of protection, we survived!

Paramedics had shown up to do a quick inspection before they were on their way. We cancelled the sleepover that night, but went to bed in our own homes, grateful to see another day. When I was 14, I had my first dream (of 4) regarding ISIS, or as we say in Arabic, Daesh. I also engaged heavily in ministry through the avenues of discipleship and teaching English as a second language. Around my high school graduation in 2009, the Lord prompted me to prophetically speak what He was showing me or relaying to my spirit into the atmosphere. I have been prophesying since then, not realizing what the next few chapters of my life would bring and how the Lord would radically transform my life in such a magnificent way. But, more hardship would come my way before the Lord would step in at the midnight hour! His timing is perfect, and He receives all the glory! In my early 20's, and during my third year (roughly) of college, I was dating this guy. Now, looking back on that time, I came to realize that he was a narcissist.

The first couple months, what we would call the honeymoon stage, were great. He was very sweet, and we went on dates every week. He came and supported me at several of my public speaking engagements, and he even offered the opportunity to speak at his church on multiple occasions. However, after a few short months, he flipped the switch and became downright mean. *Cue domestic violence.* Over the course of our relationship, his toxic behavior would escalate. He insulted me at every opportunity and gas-lighting was an all-too-common tactic he used when I tried to defend myself or to confront him about his behavior. He also refused to defend me in front of his family and friends. His family never fully accepted me because I was not of the same race. They sought to break my spirit in a rather passive aggressive way. My ex-boyfriends' friends always cracked mean-spirited jokes or spoke such harsh word curses against me. He joined in with them and came into agreement with those word curses. During one visit with his friends, I called out the toxic behavior that one of his friends was displaying at the time and this friend promptly kicked me out of the house. Mind you, this friend lived out in the middle of nowhere and the nearest gas station was 50 miles away. At that point, I made the decision to walk home.

It was not until the second mile that my (ex) boyfriend drove his car down to meet me. I continued to walk for another half mile because he angrily instructed me to get in the car. We drove back into town, and he dropped me off at home. Later that week, the love-bombing reared its head again. Another tactic that feeds into the cycle of domestic violence. My partner would purchase nice gifts or flowers for me as a way to say, "I'm sorry." On dates where it was just the two of us, he would take me to all my favorite places or create fun adventures and I felt like I was on the top of the world once again. It was all done behind a spirit of manipulation and narcissism; to keep me coming back into the same cycles with the hope that things would change. Over a year passed, and his family invited me to go camping in Ludington. I thought that it would be great to get away and we could enjoy all that nature had to share with us. In the first few days, we spent our time hiking or going swimming in the lake nearby. The weather was beautiful; the birds were singing fresh melodies. Along one of the trails, we also stumbled upon a small gift shop where he purchased a pair of sweatpants for me. Towards the last few days of our trip, his parents would make the biggest breakfast; eggs, sausage, and over 2 pounds of bacon. And it was all cooked over the fire.

That day, my partner and I had planned to traverse through other trailheads that wound throughout the campsite. I loved every moment because nature is my happy place, and the melodies of the birds bring joy to my heart. When we returned to the campsite, I went to take a short nap. Only a short time later, my (ex)boyfriend came into the trailer. He laid down right next to me and at first, I did not think too much about it until he decided (without my consent) to breach my boundaries. He proceeded to unbutton my jeans and stick his hand into my vagina. I woke up with a start and immediately asked, "What the hell are you doing?" He tried to play the victim and gaslight me by saying, 'I'm not doing anything." I laid back down on the bed and felt completely violated. A few moments pass before he seeks to take advantage of me again. This time, it was with more force, as he quickly stripped me of my clothing and positioned his full weight on me. He had removed his pants prior to getting on top of me. I was trying to fight back but I had no chance.

He had bound my wrists at the top of the bed and told me to "stop fighting." Of course, I continued to fight back but he continued to hold my wrists in a bind with one hand, and his other hand was placed over my mouth. He threatened me and told me to keep quiet as he raped me repeatedly. Time stood still. Meanwhile, his family is sitting outside the trailer, and they have no idea what is happening inside. After his heinous actions had come to an end, he gathered himself together and walked outside. I heard my (ex)boyfriend talking with his family as if everything was normal. I chose to stay where I was as my body laid there in shock. I found it difficult to process what had just taken place. Had I been in the right frame of mind, I would have quietly and secretly tried to find the gift shop so I could dial 911 and make a police report. That report was never made. Months later, he would take advantage of me again, this time, it was in my own home. In the living room, he forced me down to the ground. Though my brain wanted to say no over and over again, my body went limp and as a means of coping, I dissociated from the event until it was over. Again, my (ex)boyfriend had acted as if nothing was wrong. He did not read my body language but that did not matter. He kissed me goodbye and walked out the door. You would have thought that I would make a report this time, right? I did not make a report. Instead, I kept this secret to myself for close to a decade.

Unfortunately, in America, rape culture is all too prevalent.

Statistically, rape and sexual assault victims are not believed, and therefore, many rape and sexual assault incidents go unreported. Then there is the shame and the feeling of dirtiness to overcome. You have just been violated in the most heinous way. What do you do now? For me personally, I had to grieve over the loss of my purity. My body had been wracked with shame and that feeling of dirtiness. The feeling that you are damaged goods now. But God had a plan to restore what had been stolen from me! Just a few short months later, I made the risky decision to break up with my boyfriend. It was the day after my birthday. Those of you who have been through domestic violence know that the time after a toxic relationship has ended, is the most dangerous time for that person. That is, if they manage to escape at all.

I waited 3 agonizing weeks, because I fully believed (and still do) that he was capable of murder. I thought my ex-boyfriend would surely end my life. Thankfully, he never showed up to my home ever again. The rest of that year was uneventful until December. Before the start of this next trial, I maintained a very busy schedule. I was a full-time college student. I had a full-time internship in which I had the privilege to work with refugee families. And I was involved in 5 different ministries, 4 of which, I was honored to hold a leadership position! Through all the trauma, I thought that if I kept busy, I would not have to confront the feelings associated with everything I had been through up to that point in my life. Then December of 2013 hit. It was December 18th when I started to feel ill. I thought it was a 48-hour bug and that with a few days of rest, I could return to my responsibilities soon. It turned out to be the opposite. Each day that passed, I became more ill. On Christmas Eve morning I woke up very early. We were getting ready to go to my aunt's house for Christmas. Every time my mom shouted for me to get ready, I was laying on the bathroom floor, curled up in the fetal position and hoping to find some relief. I was also extremely nauseous and my whole body was wracked with pain. We made the decision to ride up to the hospital. They started me on an IV and gave me Dilaudid for the pain. My blood was tested for over 70 different medical conditions. All the test results were the same. They came back negative! A few hours later, I was sent home.

Over the course of a year, I was in and out of the hospital. Numerous MRIs were done, and they continued to test my blood for a myriad of medical conditions. They all came back with the same negative results. I was dying of organ failure, but the doctors couldn't pinpoint the reason. Eventually, the hospital refused to treat me. They acknowledged my symptoms but, in their mind, I was wasting valuable resources, so they sent me home. For the next few years, I continued to battle with chronic pain, nausea, and a whole host of other symptoms. I knew that I was dying, and I should be panicking but instead, I felt complete rest for the first time in my life. Odd, isn't it? Yet, in the midst of ongoing pain and borrowed time, I chose, with strength that is not my own, to look past the circumstance and rejoice.

To bask in my Saviors presence and just....simply....rest. I stayed in prayer and the Word. During this time, my prayers would fluctuate. Every few months, I would be delighted to sit before the Lord and fellowship with Him. It was so beautiful. Words cannot adequately describe all that I was feeling and experiencing. But there were days when I could smell freshly baked cinnamon bread in the spirit. Sometimes, I could smell rose oil being poured out. Still, in my humanity, I would be so wracked with pain that I would ask the Lord for relief. In the summer of 2014, I attended a barbecue. I didn't know anyone except the host. Food often made me nauseous so I could not eat very much but I sat down at one of the picnic tables. A gentleman sat down across from me and asked me how I was doing or if I had any plans for the summer. I told him that I had no plans for the summer and that, quite frankly, my health was deteriorating. He told me that I should drive down to a healing center in Kentucky. People would welcome me and pray over me. I would be healed. I looked at him with a puzzled look and mentioned that I was in no condition to drive to Kentucky.

Prior to that gathering, I had watched a video where an evangelist had listed a video. It was not like his other videos but in this particular one, he was speaking about healing. And as a child of God, healing is part of your inheritance. After I left that barbecue, I went before the Lord, and I made a bargain with Him. I said to Him, "Take me or heal me. I don't care which one." I was so desperate for relief, but I continued to praise the Lord despite it all. I contacted a local deliverance ministry, but they did not return my phone call. Fast forward to the following year! It was the spring of 2015, and I was set to graduate from college. I attended the ceremony, but you would have never known, by looking at me, that I was dying from organ failure. I was still believing for my healing at this point, but I left the decision up to God. All along, He was answering my prayers. In August of that same year, the deliverance ministry that I had previously contacted got in touch with me and asked if I was available for a deliverance session. I said yes and we set the date for September 30th. When that day came around, I showed up 40 minutes early. I used that time to commune with the Lord and prepare my heart for what was about to take place. I went in at the appointed time.

I sat down with the ladies and expressed what I wanted from the Lord. After some small talk, we allowed the Lord to do his work. I was delivered and set free from suicide, fantasy, torment, resentment, and abandonment. As soon as the demonic spirits left my body, I received my healing miracle for which I had so earnestly prayed for. All the pain, Gone! All the nausea, Gone! Every lingering symptom, Gone! But I would not recognize my healing until the very next evening. I went to Applebee's later that night for dinner, and I could smell food again without feeling nauseous. When I communed with the Lord before going to bed, I asked the Lord, "Did You heal me?" and He said, "Yes!" Out of curiosity, I asked the Lord, "Why couldn't the doctors find anything?" and the Lord responded, "The reason why the doctors couldn't find anything was because it was a spiritual problem that manifested in the physical." In other words, I had let unforgiveness settle into my heart and it almost killed me. So, I say to you, do not let unforgiveness settle into your heart. You will only poison yourself. Forgive those who have hurt you. It does not mean that you are letting them off the hook. It simply means that you are choosing to let go of the hurt and pain so that you can move forward." Soon after my first deliverance, I connected with a church.

I got baptized in 2016 and continued to walk out my first deliverance by studying the Word and getting involved with a community of like-minded believers. A few years later, when the church closed, I started to work out my own salvation with the help of Holy Spirit. I didn't fully know what God had planned for me next, but He continues to transform my life in the most marvelous of ways. In the fall of 2020, I started a mentorship led by my dear friend Hazem, one of the most insightful human beings whom I have ever known. Slowly but surely, my mindsets and my outlook on life started to change. That mentorship brought me to where I am today. God started me on a path that is beyond my wildest imagination and with each year that passes, it is only going to expand and get better! I currently work at a bookstore, and we had a beautiful woman of God enter the store that day. God had set up a divine appointment. Her name is Dawn, and when she came to my register, I asked if she was prophetic. She said yes, and my spirit resonated within me that she was a prophet.

She confirmed this and it led to my own prophetic journey. I had asked Holy Spirit to teach me all about the prophetic and now, I was ready to dive in deeper and activate what the Lord had been teaching me and what He had deposited within me. The truth of the matter is my giftings and my call were already activated many years ago, but I had not paid attention until this divine appointment changed the course of my life.

Later on, Prophetess Dawn would call me and ask if I wanted to attend a prophetic meeting. At first, and I'll be honest, I did not want to go. However, the Lord kept pressing it upon my spirit that I needed to attend this prophetic gathering. I finally relented, and from that moment on, I have continued to press forward into everything that the Lord has for me. Lo and behold, it was through this prophetic community that the Lord has provided me with a spiritual covering through Prophet Ken, who is my spiritual father. I have finally found my tribe, and as I continue to be trained and equipped to do the works of the Kingdom, I see, ever so clearly, the hand of God and His demonstrative power and redemption within my story. To rise from a pit of ashes and move into such glorious light!

I had my second deliverance in August (2022) and Jesus has been so faithful. Out of that deliverance, the Lord began to pull back the layers and set me free from shame, guilt, condemnation, feelings of unworthiness or dirtiness, self-harm, and sexual sin, which I fell into as a means of punishing myself for all the rapes and sexual assaults that transpired over many years and by multiple men. I do not mention all of them in this short excerpt, but it has been the biggest battle to overcome. What I can tell you is that, as I continue to walk out my deliverance, the Lord has walked with me every step of the way. He has increased my faith, and when the enemy comes to whisper lies, I must be diligent and not partner with those lies. I choose to believe and speak the truth of who God says I am and to walk in that identity. What Jesus has done for me; He can also do for you! Call out to Him! As we have now entered 2023, I am excited for all that God is going to do, not only for myself, but for all those who are within my sphere of influence. As I have stepped into my prophetic identity, I welcome the process and the preparation that comes with it.

Friends, healing is messy, but it is also so freeing when you begin to view life with a different but fresh lens. Give yourself permission to take that next step in your own healing journey and do not be afraid to ask for help along the way! 2023 is a big year for healing to transpire. I can feel it in my spirit and deep within my bones, to continue pressing forward in what the Lord has called to me do, in full measure and action, for the glory of His Name. It is due to the paths which I have walked, that I resonate with Iranians so personally, especially Iranian women. The circumstances are similar or equally felt but the perpetrator(s) of evil and cruel barbarity are different. I fell in love with the Iranian people around the Christmas season in 2007.

I picked up a copy of *Cry of Iran* which was written and produced by brother Haik Hovsepian's sons. From that moment on, something stirred within me. The following year (January 2008), I began reaching out to Iranians and creating friendships that were built upon love and trust. Fast forward to 2009, when I started prophesying over the nation of Iran, not recognizing my prophetic call to the nations until many years later. Many of those friends whom I connected with early on, are still in contact with me today and many more friendships have blossomed along the way. Iranians are so disillusioned with Islam and as a result, thousands are turning away from it each year! In its' place, they are seeking two kinds of freedom; a restoration of freedom in the natural world that permeates the nation and impacts their way of living and spiritual freedom that can only come through Christ. At the time of this writing, the Lord has brought restoration to my family in various contexts. I have now stepped into the prophetic call upon my life, and I continue to minister to Iranians on a regular basis, to prophecy over the Iranian homeland, and to patiently wait upon the Lord as I navigate what He has called me to fulfill within Iran and among the nations as a whole.

For much of my ministry with Iranians, I did not choose to share my story. I wanted the focus to be on them and what they wanted to receive. For some, the Lord wanted to bring healing; for others, He wanted to bring restoration. And still, for others, the Lord set them free through the action of deliverance. It was not until the fall of 2020 when I began to take another leap of faith and start fully embracing the healing process. While stepping into this messy process, I am receiving fresh waves of healing each day. Over the past couple years, I have shared my story in pieces. I believe, as more healing transpires, that the Lord will encourage me to share my story more fully so that many others (whether Iranian or non-Iranian) can receive their freedom too.

For as long as I have been involved in ministry, I find common ground when I meet people. Often, I have been down the very same roads and experienced the same struggles of those whom God places in my path. As God begins ministering through me, I am often reminded to share with people that I know exactly where you are coming from, or the feelings that you are battling with and the Lord wants to bring healing to those areas of your life that have been broken. Just a few months ago, as I was ministering among a group of Iranians, I met a young woman named *Amal.* I had received prophetic insight that she was one {of many} who struggled with shame and the feelings of worthlessness or dirtiness as a result of repeated incidents of rape and sexual assault. As the Lord began the work of setting her free, He spoke to her heart and said, "*Daughter, you are not dirty. You are precious in My sight.*" It was in that moment that *Amal* was able to fully accept her freedom and move forward into the prophetic destiny that God has planned for her. She was seen and valued. She is loved, and so are you the reader. What He did for me, for *Amal*, for many others, He can do for you!! Come with an open heart, with the faith of a child and receive what He has for you. Place your burdens upon the shoulders of Jesus. Let Him change your ashes to beauty and step into everything the Lord has for you!

"Prophetic encouragement for Iranians."

Your nation is yours; it belongs to you. It does not belong to the regime, though they be deceived in their thinking. With the latest revolution, I sympathize with you as many of you are weary. Maybe some of you are wondering if you can handle one more day or take one more step. I assure you that you can take that next step. You can put one foot in front of the other, one day at a time. Please know that you are seen. You are loved. You are valued. You are not forgotten. Though the media and the feminists are silent and the regime (IRGC included) are doing everything to keep your voices from being heard, you must continue to raise your voice even louder. Raise your voice loud, for the whole world to hear. I know that you are tired, and I know that you are weary but *Rise Up Freedom Fighter!* You must know that you exemplify courage, and your courage does not go unnoticed. Like Moses, who had Aaron and Hur to hold up his weary arms, many of us are in the battle with you. We are standing with you in the fight for freedom. With each revolution, you are taking territory back. And freedom will come back to your nation once again.

Prophetic encouragement for the Iranian Diaspora:

The Lord says that there is a separation in the natural but there is no separation with Me. Cling to me in this hour and I will carry you. You can trust Me. Many of you have been scattered from your homeland and long to return home. Others desperately long to be with loved ones in a time where your nation is in deep turmoil. I believe that the Lord wants to restore your broken hearts and bring healing to the pain that is held within the deepest part of your soul. To those who are grieving, the Lord brings comfort to you. Reach out your hand to Him and He will meet with you. May I also remind you, that you may be away from your homeland at this current time, but your voice matters.

Do not believe the lie that you are not doing enough or that you are not qualified to speak. Within your sphere of influence, let your voice be known.

Prophetic encouragement for the Persian Church:

God sees you. He sees your steadfastness. He sees your faithfulness. So as the Persian Church continues to grow and expand – so your assignment(s) will expand because you are trustworthy. You have been found faithful, even in the midst of hardship. The Lord your God will fight for you in battle. Cling to Him for your strength.

Prophetic Decrees and Deliverance:
· I speak freedom over the nation of Iran. I prophecy that everything that was stolen from you – everything that plundered – will be returned to you in full measure – in Jesus' name.
· I decree and declare that joy will be returned to you again; that tragedy would be turned into triumph; that broken hearts would be restored – in Jesus' name.

· I break off every assignment from the enemy – that came in with the regime – over the land of Iran now – in Jesus' name.
· Every trauma bond that came in with the regime – I break that off your life now and I command all spirits attached to the trauma bond – to go now – in Jesus' name.

· Every trauma bond that came in during childhood – I break that off your life now and I command all spirits attached to the trauma bond to go now – in Jesus' name.

· I break off and command the spirits of guilt and shame to leave your life now – in Jesus' name.

· I break off and command all generational curses to leave your life now – in Jesus' name.
· I break off and command every word curse that was spoken over your life – to leave your life now – in Jesus' name.

· I break off and command every spirit of death and the spirit of suicide to leave your life now – in Jesus' name.

· I break off and command the spirit of heaviness to leave your life now in Jesus' name.

· I speak and release the joy of the Lord.
· I speak and release freedom to you – in Jesus' name.
· I speak and release peace over you now – in Jesus' name.
· I speak and release comfort over you now – in Jesus' name.
· I speak and release the healing balm of Gilead over you now in Jesus' name.

· I speak and release life and abundance over you – in Jesus' name.
Prayer:

Father, I humbly come before Your Throne, and I lift up every single person who is holding this book in their hands or reading it via other means of technology. Lord, I ask you to bless them, to bless their homes, to bless their families, to bless their places of employment. I release peace over their minds now in Jesus' name. Where this is grief or sorrow, I release an overflow of joy now in Jesus' name. Where there is tragedy, I speak triumph in Jesus' name. Those who are in a season of success, I pray that you continue show favor upon their lives Lord. Father, I lift those who are reading this book, but they do not know you. They have not entered a covenant relationship with You yet. Lord, reveal yourself to them and meet with them in a very powerful and tangible way. I pray that my testimony would shine as a beacon of your light, your power, your glory, that you offer hope to the hopeless, and comfort to the broken-hearted. You specialize in bringing beauty out of the ashes. Lord, I bring before you the nation of Iran. I ask, Lord, that You embrace the Iranian people as only you can. Let healing and restoration come in like a flood. Let the Iranian people know that You have not forgotten them and that they can turn to You in their time of distress. I thank You in advance for the victory that you're going to bring. Even now, Lord, you are bringing healing and restoration to the Iranian people.

And when the regime crumbles, that healing and restoration will be even more glorious as Your power is made known across the land; allowing freedom to flow throughout the nation, allowing prosperity to return to the nation. I speak and release the healing balm of Gilead over Iran now – in Jesus' name. I cast down strongholds across the landlord, and I speak into a greater future that You have planned for her people – in Jesus' name. Amen.
Prayer of Salvation:

Jesus, I cry out to you now. I come humbly before you Lord and I repent of my sins. I believe that you died on the cross for me and rose again on the third day. I choose to accept your free gift of salvation and I ask that you would be Lord and Savior of my life. Thank you for desiring to enter into a personal relationship with me. I surrender my life to you. In Jesus' name, I pray. Amen.
Prayer of Deliverance:

Jesus, I come to you – believing that you will bring healing and deliverance to my body, mind, and soul. I forgive all those who have hurt me or caused me pain. You are welcome to say those names out loud and what they have done. I renounce _______ (list spirits that you are afflicted with) in Jesus' name. I command the spirit of _______ to leave my body now and go back to the abyss in Jesus' name. I break agreement with every generational curse, every word curse, every contract, and all legal rights – in Jesus' name. I bind and cast out any spirits that are known and unknown in Jesus' name. I break agreement with every assignment that Satan has or may have over my life – in Jesus' Name. Holy Spirit, I ask that You would fill me now; that You would show me how to walk in a covenant relationship with you.

Final Word:

As I continue to step deeper into my calling, the Lord has been so faithful to be with me every step of the way. I am humbled that the Lord continues to show me His grace as I seek and learn to rightly discern everything that He shows me or wants to speak to me. Concerning Iran, the Lord has shown me glimpses of Iran's future. When the regime finally crumbles, I strongly believe in my spirit, that the Lord desires to bring healing and deliverance across Iran.

It will also become more prevalent within the Church in Iran because that is your inheritance, and the Lord wants you to step into the fullness of everything that He has for you. Even now, in the midst of much turmoil, the Lord is doing His work and providing that healing to those who are seeking it! To the precious Iranian people, I say to you, that your nation will rise again. Your vindication is coming, and the future of your nation is brighter than what you can see in this current time and season. The nation of Iran has been prophetically claimed for good things.

Whether you are Iranian or not – and you have read this far, please know that I love you and Jesus loves you even more than I do. If you prayed either one of the prayers above or would like to receive prophetic encouragement and prayer through various social media avenues, you can connect with me through email at *heather.langerak@gmail.com*. Specifically, if you prayed the prayer for deliverance, it is important that you maintain your deliverance through the reading of His Word and connecting with a body of believers who can encourage you and edify you as you walk with Christ. Now, in Iran, this can be rather difficult so exercise wisdom but hold onto a courageous sense of boldness as well. If you are

Iranian, I would welcome the opportunity to hear from you! God bless you friends!

A Poem for Jina Mahsa Amini

The Moon was veiled in darksome cloud
She was dimmed as evil blows abound
Flowing locks sparked the tyrant's ire
Her passing shadow lit a nation afire.

The failing light of the moon that night
Foreshadowed the yearning of Aryan might
Gathering clouds of voices strong
Would bring out a massive throng.

Cries mingled with wailing lament
And tears unending the angry vent
As the moon seemed to be extinguished
She lives on in the hearts of a nation anguished

Her spirit is rising with vigor anew
The land of the lion and sun once knew
The people heard the cries of the moon
Together, with one heart, freedom looms.

(Constance Richard Parr)

Human beings are members of a whole,
In creation of one essence and soul.
If one member is afflicted with pain,
Other members uneasy will remain.
If you've no sympathy for human pain,
The name of human you cannot retain.

*Saadi, (13th century Persian poet)

Sarina Esmailzadeh
"Hello friends, Welcome to my world."
By Heather Joy

Sarina Esmailzadah woke up for school, as she did every morning. She took a shower, got dressed, and crimped her hair, to prepare for the day ahead. While it is mandatory for women in Iran to wear the hijab, she rarely wore it. She jumped in her parents' car, ready for a great day! When Sarina showed up to the school grounds, she grabbed her school bag and jumped out of the car. *"Khodahafez"* {*Goodbye*} as she looks back and waves at her brother. Her friends met her at the door. They greeted each other as they walked to their first class. Towards the end of the day, Sarina looked forward to creating her next vlog. She was an up-and-coming social media influencer and covered a wide range of topics including cooking, art, and politics, with the intention to raise awareness to the issues that Iranians regularly face while living under such an oppressive regime.

Sarina walks into her room and grabs her camera. She brings it back into the kitchen and sets it on the counter facing her. *"Salaam Bache ha! Emroz, pitza dorost mikonim."* Sarina says in a sing-song voice. {*Hello friends! Today, we are going to cook pizza.*} Sarina grabs the dough, sets it on the counter, and begins to knead it. From the refrigerator, she grabs green peppers, mushrooms, tomatoes, and cheese. While the camera continues to roll, she grabs a knife from the drawer and starts to cut up the mushrooms and other vegetables. Sarina talks to the camera about her friends, and the things that are currently happening in her life. The normal, the dramatic, the mundane, as a typical teenage girl who lives in Iran! When she wasn't busy filming, Sarina loved the outdoors and enjoyed taking walks with her brother, *Amir.* Nature was one of her happy places.

Sarina: *What are we doing today?*

*Amir: *Taking a walk. It's really nice outside today.*

It is sunny outside. The birds are chirping. The sky is blue, and people are walking around. A fairly regular day in Iran. Sarina gleefully wraps her arm about her brother's neck as they continue walking down the road.

****

Waking up to another day in Karaj. It was September 23,2022. Sarina woke up and performed her usual morning routine. Her phone rings as she's getting ready for school. It's her friend *Nasrin* and Sarina picks up the call.

Sarina: *Hello*
Nasrin: *Hello. How are you?*
Sarina: *Good.*
Nasrin*: Do you want to go to the protest after school?*
Sarina: *Yes, let's go.*
Nasrin: *Great. See you in 15 minutes!*

They hang up the phone. Sarina finishes putting on her make-up and grabs her shoes. Fifteen minutes pass. Nasrin (and other friends) wait in the car outside Sarina's home. Seeing their car, Sarina calls back to her mother, Khodahafez {Goodbye} and closes the door behind her. Right after English class, they drive to the location where the protest has already begun. Sarina, Nasrin, and all of their friends speedily jump out of the car and join in. *MARG BAR DICTATOR!!*

MARG BAR DICTATOR!! They all shout as they raise their fists in the air. *{Down with the dictator}*. Security forces, armed with batons are running throughout the streets. *MARG BAR DICTATOR!! MARG BAR DICTATOR!!* Protesters continued to shout. Sarina and her friends are unfazed by the chaos surrounding them.

Freedom is a fundamental right that is worth fighting for. *MARG BAR DICTATOR!!* All of a sudden, Bam! Sarina is hit in the head with a baton, with such force that she collapses to the ground. Bam! Bam! The security forces continue to beat her, and with each forceful blow, Sarina's skull shatters like broken glass. *VAISA. VAISA. {*Stop.} But the guards ignore her. Nasrin cries, *"Sarina!"* She rushes over and tries to reach where Sarina lies. Bam. Bam. Bam. The guard raises his arm with each swing of the baton as Nasrin cradles her friend in her arms. Sarina is barely conscious at this point as she lays in the middle of the street, a pool of blood surrounding her. Her shirt is soaked, her hair is matted. Security forces turn their attention to Nasrin and begin to beat her with the same force. She does her best to shield the blows that are coming directly at her. Other protesters continue shouting slogans against the Supreme Leader while others use their bodies as a shield to protect others around them and they too are met with a deadly beating by security forces. With a small window of time, and the security forces distracted, Nasrin turns to her other friends and they make the quick decision to carry Sarina from the road to the car. Sarina is in urgent need of medical care!

As Sarina is laying in the back seat, barely conscious, Nasrin tries to shake her in the hopes that she will awaken. *"Sarina."* Nasrin shouts to the driver: *Boro! Boro!* {Go!} And the driver zooms down the road. *Ba man bemoon Sarina* {Stay with us Sarina}, as Nasrin sits in the back seat, her friend splayed across her lap. Blood saturates the back of the car. Sarina is barely able to keep her eyes open. They bypass the hospital for security forces are known to continue their display of violence if protesters show up there, so they travel to a friend's home, to seek medical attention there. Due to the damage to her brain from repeated blunt force trauma to the head, Sarina goes into a seizure. *"Boro. Boro!"* Nasrin shouts as the driver continues to speed down the road. On the way to where they are going, Sarina dies. After arriving at their intended destination, Nasrin, and two other friends carry Sarina from the back seat of the car, and lay her on the sidewalk. Despite no medical training, they tried last ditch efforts to save her but it was to no avail. The homeowner raced outside to the scene but the damage to Sarina's brain was too severe. *She's gone.*

****

Nasrin calls Sarina's mother. It rings on the other end, and Nasrin's heart is racing. Sarina's mother *Zara* picks up the phone.

Zara: *Salaam.* {she has a sinking feeling in the pit of her stomach}

Nasrin: *Salaam - Mrs. Esmailzadeh?*

Zara: Yes.

Nasrin: *Man khabare badi daram.* {I have bad news} Nasrin is shaking as she holds the phone.

Zara: *Na. Na. Na. Na. {No}*

Nasrin: *Sarina koshte shode.* {Sarina was killed.} Nasrin's voice cracks.

Zara: *Na. Na. Sarina. NA.* {She wails}

Nasrin: *Mrs. Esmailzadeh, man kheili kheili moteasefane.* {I'm so sorry} Nasrin is crying.

Zara: *Ey Khoda.* {Oh God} She continues to sob.

Nasrin: We tried to do everything we could to save her. We tried.

Zara: *Ey Khoda. Na. Na. Sarina. Na. Azizam. Oh Ey Khoda.* {Oh God. No. Sarina, my baby.} Zara continues to sob.

The phone clicks off. Sarina's mother, Zara is in her home. Her body is trembling as she grapples with the news of her daughter's death. Unbeknownst to Zara, Sarina's body would be taken by the authorities.

For the next 10 days, Zara would go in search of her daughter. Deep in her grief, she would whisper, *Sarina, kojae? Azizam.* {Where are you? My baby} Each day that passes hurts more than the last, until Zara runs into security forces and shouts at them, asking them where they have taken her daughter.

Zara: "You are all criminals!" She shouts in their faces.

IRGC soldier: *"You* want to see your daughter?" He smirks. And the others do the same.

Zara: *"Yes,* please. My baby," She sobs.

The IRGC security forces would lead Zara to where they had taken Sarina's body. With the door open, she walks into the building where she is led down a dimly lit hallway. As they enter a small room at the end of the hallway, Zara confirms that it is, in fact, Sarina. Her body is lying on the cold hard floor. Zara, at the sight of her daughter runs and kneels down at her side, wailing, a sound that cannot be easily forgotten. She wraps her arms around Sarina's body and continues to sob loudly. Security forces look on with evil in their eyes and a smirk on their faces.

Zara: *SARINA. Ey Khoda.* She gasps between sobs. {Oh God} *Azizam. Ey Khoda. Na. Na. Na. Sarina.* She grasps Sarina's hand.

Eshgham man. Eshgham man, Sarina. Azizam. {I love you, my baby}
Ey Khoda. Zara repeats to herself.

Security forces continue to look on when one of the men approaches her and says, "Your daughter is immoral. She is a terrorist!" They all laugh and continue taunting Zara as she sobs over the loss of her beloved daughter. Though she does not want to leave her daughter, Zara rises to her feet in shame, and leaves the building, unable to listen to their evil laughter and constant taunting remarks.

Three days would pass and Zara finds it hard to get out of bed, knowing that she will never hear Sarina's voice again or witness Sarina's spunky personality. *Ey Khoda. Is this a dream?* She thinks to herself. At the reality that her daughter is gone, she begins to sob uncontrollably. Zara's heart is broken, shattered beyond all reason. While her husband is at work, she opens the closet door to find a stool. Her grief is unbearable. With the stool in her hand, she goes to look for a rope. When Zara finds a rope that is strong enough, she takes both items into the bedroom. She lays the rope on the bed and the stool on the ground near her bedroom closet. Her whole body is shaking and wracked with grief. *Sarina,* Zara whispers, *Ey Khoda.* She sobs so hard that she nearly loses her balance. *May God forgive me, Sarina.* She looks up with tears streaming down her face. {I love you and I miss you so much} Zara grabs the rope from the bed and secures it tightly. She pauses, contemplating what she is about to do next. She takes a step forward and steps up on the stool grabbing the rope that is now securely tied in place. Zara places the rope around her neck. She pauses one last time and sobs. Her grief consuming her, she steps off the stool and dies within a few minutes.

In one of Sarina's last videos before her death, she would speak to the camera one last time and document her thoughts on the topic of freedom. She explains to her audience that Iranians are tired of living under a repressive regime, remarking that *"My homeland feels like being in exile."* Before ending the video, questions swirl within her mind. She asks herself, *"Chera dar Iran be donya umadam?"* {Why was I born in Iran?} With a glint of hope in her eyes, and knowing the desperation of her people, Sarina thinks out loud, *"Vaghan mishe?"* {Could it be possible?} She signs off but not before telling her audience, *"Hich hesi behtar az azadi nist!* {Nothing feels better than freedom.} The IRGC (Iranian Revolutionary Guard Corp) changed Sarina's posts after her death to make it seem like she was depressed and suicidal. Nothing could be further from the truth because Sarina found a way to love her life, despite the restrictions of the regime. She sought to raise awareness of the plight of her people and the issues that Iranians face on a daily basis while living under such a dictatorial regime.

Sarina, possessing such a sweet spirit, was equally fearless and full of courage. She was willing to risk everything, including her life to change the future of her nation and create a life where Iranians could live with a better purpose and dignity. Could it really happen? Sarina asks. Yes, my sweet girl, change is coming to your nation. A day is coming when freedom will arise at last and when that day comes, your sacrifice will be remembered.

****

Reflection:

And I heard a loud voice from heaven, saying, Look! The tabernacle of God is with men and He will dwell with them. They shall be His people, and God Himself will be with them and be their God. God shall wipe away all tears from their eyes. There shall be no more death. Neither shall there be any more sorrow nor crying nor pain, for the former things have passed away. Revelation 21:3-4

Iranians, across every city and province in Iran, shout *"Azadi,*

Azadi, Azadi," a rallying cry for freedom. Friends, may I share with you that true lasting freedom is found through a personal relationship with Jesus Christ! And in His eternal Kingdom, there is no more sorrow, no more pain, no more death as Revelation 21 points out. There is coming a future for Iran where freedom will sweep the land. I believe that freedom will not just sweep the land but it will weave itself into every aspect of daily living upon the earth. A heavenly glimpse of heaven is coming to the nation of Iran where Iranians, through the power of God, are set free from all the trauma, the sorrows, the pain they have endured and are able to take a deep breath. To live with a greater dignity and purpose, where there is freedom to take a deep breath and capture every moment with renewed joy and strength. I do not know what Sarina's beliefs were, whether she held loosely to her Islamic roots or whether she had the opportunity to hear and respond to the Gospel. I will never know the answer, but after compiling a glimpse of her story, she has become like my little sister whom I never got the chance to meet.

A few days would pass, and as I went to bed one night, I saw Sarina in a dream. She was standing in a meadow and wearing a beautiful dress. She was barefoot. The sky was bright blue, with fluffy clouds. There was a slight breeze as the birds were chirping and the streams were flowing nearby. It was very warm. The sun was shining so brightly. Sarina had just picked some flowers and she brought them to her nose. Their scent was unlike anything she had ever smelled before. The atmosphere was filled with peace. Absent from the atmosphere was violence, pain, and death. Her body was made whole. As she continued to smell the flowers, she looked up at the sky, and heard the crisp sound of the birds as they sang their beautiful melodies. A robed figure, dressed in white, walks through the meadow. Just before He (Jesus) approaches her, Sarina turns around. And when she does, Jesus extends His hand to her. She graciously clasps her hand in His, and He twirls her. Sarina has a big smile on her face! When Jesus looks at her, He smiles too. They continued to dance in the meadow without a care in the world!

Laughter and joy abounded in an atmosphere that was created with perfection! Peace filled the air, and the dream would end.

This picture is a beautiful representation of how Jesus longs to embrace you, the reader, in a covenant relationship with Him. An eternity with Him that will last a lifetime!

<u>Armita Abassi</u>
"Living with the scars."

On February 7, 2023, 22-year-old Armita Abbasi was finally released from prison on bail after 120 grueling days in captivity. The platinum blonde freedom fighter finally emerged from the "hell hole" of Fardis Prison in Karaj with her hair now fully grown back. She emerged as a survivor bearing the ugly scars of horrific sexual abuse by the vile security forces that had arrested her. It is a well-known fact that in Iran, women are treated as nothing more than objects of sexual pleasure, to satisfy the male predators that stalk them on a daily basis. It was during the early months of the uprising that security forces raped their female prisoners as one way of silencing them and putting an end to the protests. They chose the women that were pretty and ones that suited their pathetic appetite. Once such woman was Armita Abbasi.

Armita grew up in the city of Karaj and was a regular on social media. She loved to get on Instagram and make videos of herself drinking coffee and playing with her cats. However, Armita was also well known as a bold and courageous leader of the protests. When she wasn't on Instagram, she was busy in the city streets speaking out against the government oppression of women.

On October 10, Security forces finally converged on Armita and arrested her while she was protesting in the streets. According to one eyewitness, she was beaten and thrown into a state security van, where she was brutally gang raped on the way to jail. Eight long and grueling days passed and on October 17, Armita was rushed to Imam Ali Hospital in Karaj by plainclothes officers. When she arrived, doctors noted that her head was shaved. She was shaking violently and hemorrhaging from the rectum. Within a few hours, security forces secretly removed her from the rear entrance of the hospital before her parents could see her. The doctors who examined Armita were convinced that she had been sexually assaulted. However, the official report from the police was that Armita was suffering from a hemorrhoidal condition prior to her arrest.

Since the Iranian Revolution, when Khomeini was the Supreme Leader, it had been a common practice for female prisoners to be sexually molested and raped to keep them from entering paradise after they are executed. The Supreme Leader declared, "Such rapes are essential to prevent these "Anti-Islamic" women from entering paradise. So, rape is extremely important to prevent them from entering heaven."

A vile religious practice to satisfy the disgusting appetite of pathetic men is performed on helpless, innocent women, so instead of going to paradise, they will suffer for eternity in hell. This is exactly how Armita was treated. She was pretty, intelligent, and a threat to the male establishment. They could not tolerate her being a leader of the protests, for having Molotov cocktails in her home, and for daring to stand up against the government. She had to be punished and taught a lesson. Her family was also warned not to talk to the media. They were told, "If you want to see your daughter alive again, you need to participate in a TV interview, saying that their daughter was taken to the hospital due to "bloody diarrhea," and not rape. However, her family refused.

On January 2, 2023, Armita went on a dry hunger strike in prison, protesting her long detention and lack of medical care. Fourteen other cellmates joined in. A few weeks later, Armita's lawyers resigned from her case, stating that they were not allowed to visit their client in person. A court appointed lawyer stepped in and took her case. A week later, Armita was brought before Judge Assef Al-Hosseini, who is known for his cruelty, and was charged with "propaganda against the establishment, making Molotov cocktails, and holding a gathering with the intention of acting against national security." The charges against Armita are serious enough to put her behind bars for an extremely long time.

Armita is out on bail but she is forced to live with the traumatic scars of extreme sexual abuse. The images of the horrendous rape attack haunts her in the sleepless nights where she lies awake struggling to suppress the nightmares! I cannot even imagine what she is going through! The psychological and spiritual damage that was done to Armita's body and mind is utterly unacceptable!

Dear Armita, My heart aches for you. I know you are a tough, brave, and very strong woman, but you bear the scars of vile predators determined to punish you for life for standing up to a dictatorship government. I admire your incredible courage, Armita. I want to share with you that there is a loving God that desires to heal the trauma and the scars that you are suffering from. When you were terrified and shaking with fear, He was there to comfort you. He is a God of compassion and love, Armita. There is a beautiful promise in the Bible written just for you. It says, *"You keep track of all of my sorrows. You have collected all my tears in your bottle. You have recorded each one in your book."* (Psalm 56:8)

Dear Armita, Jesus understands your pain and suffering, He experienced horrific pain while he was dying on the cross to forgive all of our guilt and shame. For every tear that you cried and every pain that you endured, God kept track of it. He recorded it in his book and I assure you dear Armita, that those who violated you will be held accountable. They will not escape justice. Cry out to Jesus, dear Armita. He is waiting for you with his arms of love held open wide to bring hope and healing to your scars.

<u>Reflection</u>
By Heather Joy

Armita has been released from captivity and placed on bail. After her release, she smiles. Behind that smile, there is pain. Pain that runs deep to the core of her soul and that of my own as well. I am also a survivor of rape and sexual assault. I was known as the "happy-go-lucky" person in public. People wondered how I could be so happy and honestly, it was the grace of God over my life. He is the one who sustained me. What people didn't see is everything that happened behind the scenes. I faced the greatest mental health battle of my life. *The tears. The doubt. The shame.* The feeling of "dirtiness." The thoughts of suicide. My mind took me to some really dark places. I kept everything a secret for a decade. Every time that someone took advantage of me in a sexually vulgar way, I wanted to retreat deeper and deeper into my shell, my hiding place. I had no one to turn to and I could not afford therapy on my low-level income so I turned to poetry to release my thoughts and inner turmoil. In my own journey towards healing and wholeness, I finally worked up the courage to use my voice and speak in the fall of 2021, to finally talk about what had been kept hidden for so long. As time moves on, I continue to receive more levels of healing and wholeness.

The Lord continues to restore what was so violently taken away from me; to touch my pain with the healing balm of His grace and love! By the power of God, I have been set free! I am currently unaware of the level of resources in Iran, when it comes to trauma, but I can imagine Armita's thoughts as she works through her own healing journey. My heart longs for her to find someone she can trust and release her deepest hurts. I can only pray that Armita does not keep silent for as long as I did, but that she finds freedom in the midst of her most painful battle. May she seek and cry out to Jesus, allowing Him to embrace her through this journey towards healing, just as He did for me. He longs to embrace her and set her free! I resonate with her so strongly because she is most likely digesting and processing the same emotions I have worked through. Armita is a courageous woman who has endured so much. Her joyous smile will touch the hearts of many as she rises from the ashes of her captivity.

Armita and I, though we are 7000 miles apart, have faced the deeply painful consequences of such heinous actions which were committed at the hands of others but I am here to tell you that this is not the end of our story! *This is not the end of your story.* God can redeem you, from even the darkest of pits! If you know someone who is a survivor of rape or sexual assault, {maybe they come to you for help} please believe us. That is the greatest gift you can give us as we begin the healing process.

Reader, whatever storm or trial you are going through, take the time to heal. I promise you that it is worth it. Sometimes, it might be more painful than the initial event, but you have the courage to rise again. Stand to your feet. Each day is a new gift that is given to us. Take one step at a time; do not try to figure out everything all at once. And it is perfectly okay if you take one step forward and 10 steps back as you continue to process the levels of trauma in your own life. Keep moving forward. Healing is a messy process but it is also so freeing. *There is freedom. There is joy.* Your suffering is not your identity, it can lead to the beginning of a bright future. Be courageous. Step out of the dark and let your own healing journey begin. Jesus, set the captives free!

Armita, sweet girl! One day, justice will come. Your suffering is not in vain. Speak boldly!

<u>Toomaj Salehi</u>
Truth-teller: a voice that cannot be silenced.
"If you're not in the fight {for freedom} with us, then don't bother fighting for my release."
<u>Heather Joy</u>

Toomaj woke up at the sound of his alarm. It was 8am in the beautiful city of Isfahan. Toomaj pulled back the covers, went to his closet, and picked out his outfit for the day. Then, he walked to the bathroom where he brushed his teeth and took a shower. Fifteen minutes later, he put on his clothes and walked to the dining room. He pulled out one of the chairs from the dining room table and put on his favorite pair of sneakers. Toomaj grabbed his keys and wallet before heading out to his day job where he worked as a welder at a metal factory. Although Toomaj was a top-notch employee and enjoyed the company of his fellow co-workers, his truest passion is music. His rap lyrics speak of the injustice and oppression that Iranians have suffered under such a corrupt and notoriously wicked regime.

In addition to his musical career, Toomaj has maintained a strong social media presence. When you listen to his words, he makes you think about things from a different perspective. It is not surprising that Toomaj has a large following and thousands continue to be inspired by him. He is a strong leader and has a compassionate heart. I personally believe, deep in my heart, that Toomaj has a prophetic calling upon his life. He has yet to discover it but in due time, he shall step into it. On his personal accounts, he sought to bring encouragement to his fellow Iranians. He would stress the importance of unity and caring for one another. One day, I randomly stumbled upon one of his videos, and in it, Toomaj proclaimed that *"this country is ours; it belongs to the people."* I decreed these exact words!!! What a prophetic confirmation to the things that the Lord has spoken to me, concerning Iran and her precious people! The land of Iran has been prophetically claimed for good things! Like Toomaj, many Iranians are trailblazers, who are forging a new path towards freedom. Behind the scenes, I believe that the Living God is creating a new future for the Iranian people that is more glorious than what is seen in this current season of turmoil.

As a prominent figure with a significant platform, media outlets would request interviews with him and Toomaj would often discuss the plight of his nation, the barbarity that Iranians have suffered and continue to endure, and ways in which people {or other nations} can stand in solidarity and press {with international pressure} for regime change. In one of his interviews with a Canadian news outlet, when asked about his thoughts regarding the regime, Toomaj boldly stated, "We are dealing with a mafia that is willing to kill the entire nation to keep their power, money, and guns." Yet the regime has continued to fail in their efforts to silence Toomaj. Stretching all the way back to 2021, he would have encounters with security forces who wanted to confront him on the basis of his rap lyrics.

The following year, they subsequently arrested him on January 12, 2022, charging him with *"activities of propaganda, and inciting the Supreme Leader."* Toomaj's sentence would be deferred for 6 months and he would be released on bail as his supporters condemned his arrest. During that six-month period, Toomaj was summoned to court but he skipped his court date to write another song entitled, "Tanabe Daar" {Gallows Noose} Toomaj continued to create more song lyrics and conduct more interviews until he was arrested on September 12, 2022. The IRGC traveled to the province of Chaharmahal {in Isfahan} and barged into Toomaj's home, placing handcuffs on his wrists and shoving him outside to one of their vans. He faced the same charges but they would not stand. Nine days later, on September 21, 2022, the outcry of his supporters combined with increased international pressure led to his release, though it would be short-lived. After the unjust murder of Mahsa Amini, Toomaj joined his fellow countrymen in the streets. Between his rap lyrics, and joining the protests, the IRGC tried to paint Toomaj as a terrorist, saying *"he's a leader of the riots, and he incites violence."* I posit that the regime is fearful of truth-tellers like Toomaj. He is a leader but not in the way that he has been painted. Just a month later, Toomaj was re-arrested on October 30, 2022. They blind-folded him, placed handcuffs on his wrists, and shoved him back into one of their vans. The state media claimed that Toomaj was fleeing the country in order to tarnish his reputation even further and paint him as not only a terrorist but a coward.

Toomaj is no coward; he would not abandon his fellow Iranians as they continue to fight for freedom. After all, freedom is not a crime!

On November 26, 2022, after he had been sitting in a prison cell for some time, the Revolutionary Court held Toomaj's trial behind closed doors where he would face a different set of charges. His lawyer was barred from seeing him or providing any sort of legal defense. Instead, Toomaj was charged with *"Moharebeh"* {enemy of God} and corruption upon the earth. He is in imminent danger of being executed. As of this writing, his family has not heard from or spoken to Toomaj since his latest arrest. He is currently being held in Dastgard Prison where he has undergone severe physical and psychological torture. It has been over 100 days since Toomaj was placed in solitary confinement and he has wavered in and out of consciousness since the start of his sentence. His body has been wracked with pain. At this point in time, they have broken his ribs, making each breath nearly unbearable. They have broken one of his legs, leaving him unable to walk. Other injuries include a broken nose and fingers. Toomaj has also lost his eyesight in one eye. He has gone on a hunger strike to protest the unjust and downright cruel ways in which the regime continues to treat political prisoners.

Security forces have denied Toomaj from receiving any level of medical care, of which he is in urgent need. They are doing everything they can to break his spirit but he continues to be strong in the face of it all. To fight for his life and not back down from speaking the truth, it must be noted that psychological torture is no joke. Though he is a freedom fighter and has a strong will to survive each hardship that is thrust upon him, he is also a human being. Toomaj is struggling with the battle going on in his mind. The mental scars he carries will require much healing. Toomaj knew the risks but he has always stood his ground. He exemplifies courage and truth is important to him. Do not believe any false confessions that the regime would seek to extract from him and use as another means to promote fear. I do not believe that he would compromise the truth. In this age and hour, every evil thing will be exposed and brought to the light. For close to four decades, the regime has set themselves up as "God." However, in the {ongoing} fight for freedom, the people's courage and their bravery speaks more powerfully.

Join in this fight for freedom, for freedom is worth fighting for. *Be Toomaj's voice*, as he has been a voice for the voiceless and has inspired positive change all over the world. As for this regime, they are being exposed for everything that they are and for everything that they stand for. Their time will soon come to an end!

Maral Rostami
"Heartbroken over my homeland."

*Maral Rostami is my dearest Iranian friend. In October of 2015, Maral and her ten-year-old son, Parham, were forced to flee Iran after security forces arrived at her home to arrest her for being on social media without wearing a hijab. For over three grueling months, Maral and her son, traveled from Turkey to Germany with a refugee group, on foot across the Zagros mountains, in a leaky rubber raft in the Aegean Sea, and in buses, until they finally arrived in Germany. Today, Maral is a successful dental assistant after completing her college degree. You can read about her incredible journey in my book, *"Finding hope and a future; Maral's journey to freedom."*

In 1979, a radical Islamic sect indoctrinated the Iranian people against their government by appealing to their religious establishment under the pretext that the Shah's government had corrupted and weakened their Faith. After much protesting, they took over the government. As soon as they had established a base of power, they started killing people in masses. This created terror in the hearts of their opponents. Innocent people were put to death and many were put into prison. For the past four decades, The Islamic Republic have brutally oppressed my people.

They have corrupted my country, attacked our history, and transformed our culture from its rich Persian history to Sharia Law. They have transferred all of its capital to foreign investors. With the death of Mahsa Amini, our compatriots protested inside and outside of Iran, and I personally always believed that the revolution is not possible without bloodshed. The power and weapons are in their hands, but we are unarmed and defenseless people. The whole world is witnessing our youth every day being killed in their pursuit of democracy and freedom.

Everyday, I ask myself this question, "Why is the country, that gave the world its first declaration of human rights, (The Cyrus Cylinder) having now to struggle and die for their own freedom?

The Islamic Republic of Iran is an abnormal regime that began its rule with countless and horrific crimes.

One of the abnormal and cruel features of this regime is the oppression and isolation of women. The Hijab Law is used as a political tool to control their minds and bodies. They utilize all kinds of deception, threats, and propaganda to keep women under their control, treating them like second class citizens. All businesses are forced to only hire women that comply with the mandatory hijab requirements.

In TV and movies, all successful women are forced to wear the hijab. They must do this in order to be accepted in society. If they refuse to comply, they will lose their government benefits and be treated as outcasts.

With this behavior, they send the message to society that women who disobey are responsible for the very severe consequences that will befall them, thereby exposing women to all disrespect. They have turned society into a kind of hunting ground by releasing their agents, who have largely become sex traffickers.

The Islamic Republic's propaganda apparatus is very active, forcing women to wear the hijab using various methods of encouragement and threats. In 2014, agents from the city of Isfahan sprayed acid on women's faces to incite terror and threats.

The Islamic Republic's Hijab has very destructive effects on society. In small isolated communities among people with little knowledge, they have created a belief that women are the property of men and if they disobey, they are killed. Gender segregation in the schools has very negative consequences on boys and girls preparing for the future, resulting in abuse and a very high divorce rate. Iran has become one very big prison and my people are exhausted from the constant struggle.

My writer friend, Mr. Randy L. Noble, asked me how do I feel about the uprising in Iran? I carry pain, anger, and hope with me as I watch the news. Many days, I wake up with fear and go to sleep, praying for my homeland.

I'm scared that something bad will happen to them! I'm scared that this uprising will fail, but I'm also happy and hopeful when I see the support of people from other countries.

I know that freedom is a very valuable gift and a blessing. It is not easy to get. In the fight for freedom, many lives are lost and many sacrifices are needed. The government is killing my friends and countrymen, and I am filled with anger!

Sometimes, I am ashamed that I have not done much or cannot do much outside of my country. Despite all of this, I always have hope. Sometimes, I am full of anger. Sometimes, I am full of fear. Sometimes, I cry. Sometimes, I am silent but I am never disappointed. I have hope that one day there will be democracy and freedom for my homeland. There will be a day when Iranians can finally rest from their struggle.

In The name of the god of the rainbow
Paymaneh Sabet

*Paymaneh has been my dear Iranian friend for more than eight years. She is a refugee living in Malaysia. One day she hopes to be given a new homeland where she can worship and live in peace. Paymaneh is a gifted writer and journalist. She has written stories about the struggles of Iranians for my podcast, "The Cross in the Desert." Paymaneh also works as a translator.

"Ice again. This damn ice."

This is the sentence many Iranians say with tears in their eyes when they see ice these days. The ice that makes drinks pleasant for millions of people brings heartbreaking memories to millions of Iranians, memories that will not fade out for years.

It started with the story of *Kian Pir-Falak,* the genius boy who was born in 2013 and was shot to death by security forces in his father's car on Nov. 16, 2022. He did not have a chance to complete his journey here on this earth, even for only a decade.

Kian's relatives: *Do you have ice.*

Neighbors: Yes. *How much do you need?*

Kian's relatives: *As much as possible. All of it, if you don't need it.*

Neighbors: *Oh. The Pir-Falaks must have a lot of guests...*

Millions know Kian from the video of him testing his hand-made boat hoping to become a robotics engineer one day in the future. Many mourn for his dashed hopes. But not everyone knows that the family had to place his little chubby body on the ice at home instead of a morgue. Why ice? The family was afraid his body would be stolen by security forces. In many cases, it has happened that the security forces either buried the bodies secretly or asked the families for a huge amount of money after stealing their victims' bodies. In many cases, they even called the prisoners' families informing them that they had executed their loved ones and buried them in silence. They denied any last meetings before execution.

****

Hamed Salahshour was a 23-year-old taxi driver. Security forces claimed that he died from a heart attack. This was a lie. He was murdered at the hands of security forces while he was in custody. He also showed shocking signs that he had undergone a surgical procedure. His family did not have a chance to hide his body in ice because he was in the security forces' hands and was buried at night-time far from his home. Why? Was it because they did not want the family to see the signs of something beyond torture? They never expected his body to be taken out and observed.

"His face was smashed. His nose, jaw, and chin were broken. His torso from his neck to his navel, and over his kidneys, was stitched up. After they exhumed his body, which had been wrapped in plastic and covered in blood, his relatives wanted to bury him in another place.

****

Dr. Aida Rostami, along with some other medical students, visited and treated injured protesters at home since the regime had kidnapped injured protesters from hospitals. Security guards claimed that Aida was killed in an accident but this is not true. The security forces brutally murdered her for simply offering medical aid to her people. The body her family saw looked totally different. She had a smashed face, broken arms, an enucleated left eye with stitches on it, and some bruises on the body. It was then that people became aware of a tragedy, an unbelievable crime, and found out why young people were kidnapped from hospitals. Some questions were answered. Many strong and healthy athletes were executed and secretly buried. Their organs were sold in order to fill the pockets of the terrorists. Though the regime would force the families to pay for the bullets which were shot at their loved ones, they would continue to sell the organs of their victims. In fact, they did not kill them because of the protests, but because of their valuable organs.

Now the question is, was Navid Afkary killed for the same reason? Navid was a star athlete who won many gold medals. When he died, his family was only allowed to see his face. They were not permitted to see his body during the burial. Why was the cloth, which his body had been wrapped in and carried to the burial, stained with blood from the inside?

What about Reyhaneh Jabbari? Her family was only allowed to see her face. They were not permitted to see the rest of her body either. What about the hundreds of prisoners who were buried in secret and only their faces were shown to the families? How much money was made from selling their organs? How was the surgical procedure conducted? Were they human enough to give their victims anesthesia? Were they human enough not to scare their victims by telling what was going to happen to them? And another serious question, "Do those who buy the organs know where the organs are coming from?"

Such a tragedy! People pay to buy an organ and live for a few more years. Meanwhile, the regime in Iran kills people and makes money off of their remains.

They killed Kian. In honor of Kian, the school would change its name *to Kian Pir-Falak School.* There was another play center and the regime commanded the owner change the name of his establishment. The name of the center was Rangin Kaman (colorful bow meaning rainbow) What's wrong with the name? in one of his videos, Kian started his experiment and tested his boat. He named his boat, "God of the rainbow." This video went viral and that made the government scared of the term, "rainbow." Now when Iranians see a *rainbow,* and a boat we will remember Kian. When we see *a hairband,* we will remember Hadis Najafi tying her hair for the last time in the video. When we see a *microphone,* we will remember Nika. When we see martial arts or a knife, we will remember Mohammad Hosseini, the martial art coach who was executed for having the things he was carrying to train his students. Who can eat pizza without feeling suffocated remembering the handsome and energetic Mehrshad, the young professional chef who had a lot of talent behind the kitchen? We will remember Hamidreza Rouhi. He was an outstanding wrestler. A young man who loved to sing and ride on his motorcycle.

Iran is a strange country. Thousands of young people have lost their lives while the regime continues to hold on to power with a vise-like grip. Every morning, when we arrived at school, they forced us to chant the words, "Oh God, shorten our life, but instead, add to the life of the leader." This regime is demonic in nature!

A Prophetic word for the future of Iran

Every Sunday evening my faithful prophetic friend, Heather Joy and I, meet together to fervently pray for the nation of Iran. During our time of prayer, God will sometimes give Heather and I, a word of prophecy concerning the people of Iran. Before the completion of our book, God was faithful to give me a special word of exhortation and prophecy about the future of Iran. This is a prophetic word meant to encourage and exhort the Iranians, which is what prophecy is supposed to accomplish. (See 1 Corinthians 14:1-3) The word that the Lord gave to me is based on two important scriptures that speak about the restoration of troubled nations, one being Israel, and the other being Elam. The Jeremiah prophecy historically applies to Israel, but I believe it can also apply, in secondary application, to any nation that is seeking after God. While the government of Iran is certainly not seeking after the God of the Bible, the underground house church of Iran, certainly is! I pray that this prophetic word will be a true blessing to all who will read it.

Jeremiah 29:11-13

"For I know the plans that I have for you," declares the Lord, "plans to prosper you and not to harm you, plans to give you a hope and a future. Then you will call upon me and come to pray to me, and I will listen to you. You will seek me and find me when you seek me with all of your heart."

Jeremiah 49:38-39

"And I will set my throne in Elam and destroy their kings and officials, declares the Lord. "But in the <u>latter days</u> I will restore the fortunes of Elam, declares the Lord."

*Elam in the Hebrew Bible, is said to be one of the sons of Shem, the son of Noah. The name *Elam* was an ancient civilization centered in the far west and southwest part of modern-day Iran. This was during the pre-Iranic period of 3200 BC.

****

Waves of My glory and waves of restoration are coming soon to your land, Oh Iran. I will break into pieces the hardened soils of death and destruction that has plagued you for more than 40 years, and will cause the "Rose of Persia" to blossom once again. Refreshment and restoration are coming back to your land. I have not forgotten you. I am breathing new life into your hearts and minds. Very soon the walls of this present evil regime will come crumbling down because of the faithful prayers of my elect. "The walls are falling; the Spirit is calling."

A corrupt leadership will soon be dissolved and a new area of peace and freedom will come into your land like a flood. My Word has promised you a hope and a future. I have promised to establish my throne and my kingdom in Elam. The church in Iran is about to rise up and conquer the evil forces that have plagued them for so long. My Spirit has given you the victory! Rise up Iran. You will no longer have to meet secretly. I have given you this land, so rise up and take it! I will summon all of the refugees from foreign lands and cause them to return to the New Iran. *I am birthing a New Iran.* Your hardship and suffering are about to be rewarded. Keep your eyes and hearts focused entirely on me. I am your only hope and reward. I will restore to you everything that the enemy has devoured and, on that day, you will worship me as the true king of Iran.

(Heather's prophetic word, concerning Iran)

In my time with the Lord, I saw what looked like a neon sign. In Persian colors, the sign said *"New Iran!"* As I pressed in further, the

Lord began speaking to my spirit and saying, *"Where all the previous revolutions brought widespread death and grief, there will come a revolution that will bring freedom across the land."* I believe that not only will freedom spread across the land but that it will also impact every aspect of daily living. The Bible says, in John 10:10, that the devil comes to steal, kill, and destroy, but Jesus says that I have come to give life, and give life abundantly. One day, the Lord was talking to me about the word abundance and He shared with me that a part of that abundance which He longs to give us and lavish upon us is freedom. Azadi! There has been soil that has been consistently prayed over and sown into. Christ is King over Iran and Iran has been prophetically claimed for good things! Behind the scenes, God is creating a new future for her that is more glorious that what you are seeing in this current season. Your nation will arise again. You, {the people}, will arise from the ashes again with fresh strength.

If you wish to contact the authors of this book:
Randy L. Noble.
rnoble1065@sbcglobal.net
Facebook page: Randy L. Noble.

Heather Joy
heather.langerak@gmail.com
Facebook page: Heather Joy.

www.ingramcontent.com/pod-product-compliance
Lightning Source LLC
Chambersburg PA
CBHW061057250726
48653CB00001B/439